Schöningh

EinFach
Englisch
Unterrichtsmodell

Series Editor: Hans Kröger

Kurt Vonnegut

Slaughterhouse-Five

by
Karola Schallhorn

edited by
Hans Kröger

Einzelarbeit
Partnerarbeit
Gruppenarbeit
Unterrichtsgespräch
Schreibauftrag
Hausaufgabe
Audio-CD
filmische Präsentation
Projekt, offene Aufgabe
kreative Aufgabe
szenisches Spiel, Rollenspiel
Internet-Recherche

Vorwort

Der Titel der Reihe **EinFach Englisch** verdeutlicht Zielsetzung und Programm zugleich. Einerseits soll Schülerinnen und Schülern auf einfache Art und Weise der Zugang zu klassischen, aber auch neuen literarischen Werken und Filmen ermöglicht werden, andererseits sollen Lehrerinnen und Lehrern in der Praxis erprobte Unterrichtsmodelle angeboten werden, die die wichtigsten methodisch-didaktischen Ansätze ihres Faches Englisch abdecken. Dabei sind die Modelle direkt, ohne langes Einlesen einsetzbar und stellen Unterrichtsarbeit konkret vor. Als besonders hilfreich für die Praxis haben sich dabei folgende Aspekte erwiesen, die für die Gestaltung der Reihe wesentlich sind:

- Überblick über **Figurenkonstellation**, ggf. **Filmszenen** und **Inhalt**
- **Klausuren** mit **Erwartungshorizont**
- **Arbeitsblätter, Tafelbilder** und **Leitfragen** für den Unterricht
- **Piktogramme** als Hinweise auf **Unterrichts**- und **Arbeitsformen**

Das Prinzip der „**Components**" ermöglicht darüber hinaus den variablen Einsatz der Modelle in unterschiedlich konzipierten Unterrichtsreihen. Dabei stehen Machbarkeit und Praxisnähe stets im Vordergrund.

Das vorliegende Modell bezieht sich auf folgende Textausgabe: Kurt Vonnegut: Slaughterhouse-Five. Published by Dell Publishing a division of Random House, Inc., New York. Copyright © 1969 by Kurt Vonnegut Jr.

Sprachliche Betreuung: Alexandra Rieb

Westermann Schroedel Diesterweg Schöningh Winklers GmbH
Braunschweig, Paderborn, Darmstadt

www.schoeningh-schulbuch.de
Schöningh Verlag, Jühenplatz 1–3, 33098 Paderborn

Druck 5 4 3 2 1 / Jahr 2017 16 15 14 13
Die letzte Zahl bezeichnet das Jahr dieses Druckes.

Umschlaggestaltung: Jennifer Kirchhof
Druck und Bindung: westermann druck GmbH, Braunschweig

ISBN 978-3-14-041163-9

Getting started

Quick Writing

- Look at the picture and jot down whatever comes to your mind. Do not stop writing until you are told to do so.

Kurt Vonnegut: Slaughterhouse-Five

The novel

The author[1]

Kurt Vonnegut Jr., died at the age of 84 on 11 April 2007 after a fall in his house in Manhattan. The *Kurt Vonnegut Memorial Library* was founded after his death to commemorate him as one of the most important but also disputed American anti-war writers. It promotes Vonnegut's self-conception as a critical writer and includes campaigns against censorship, as it is a matter of fact that *Slaughterhouse-Five* is even today banned from several schools throughout the US. Vonnegut once said "But I continue to believe that artists – all artists – should be treasured as alarm systems." He was a self-declared admonisher raising his index finger in the warning that mankind should not blow up the earth and thus destroy itself. The Museum also holds commemorative days for former POWs, especially on Armistice Day.

For his rather depressing and satirical view of society and civilization, he was run down by critics as a cynical fatalist, malcontent nihilist, and sceptic "worry-wart". His motives as a writer were definitely political. It must have been fate that he was born on 11 November 1922 which is Armistice Day – a meaningful coincidence. His nearly prophetical writings with a touch of the environmentalist in a unique style of science fiction and montage technique only received positive acclaim in retrospect.

With *Slaughterhouse-Five,* Vonnegut made an immediate breakthrough: the majority of critics praised his novel, and he won international fame. It was translated into almost all European languages. Critics praise him for being one of the best satirists and see his most lasting contribution to America's literature in his innovative style that he describes as "telegraphic-schizophrenic" due to his encounter with the Tralfamadorian aliens in the novel.

Vonnegut's idols were Jesus, Abraham Lincoln and Eugene Debs, the Labour leader who several times stood for US president as a candidate for the Socialist Party of America. In 1971, he was awarded the Master's degree in Anthropology that compensated for his failure as a young student. The American P.E.N. Club elected him as vice-president in 1972. As to his literary successes, *Jailbird* (1979) was respected as his best book after *Slaughterhouse-Five.* As a prolific writer, artist, and speaker, Vonnegut met divided critical attention.

Throughout the 1980s and 1990s, Vonnegut acted as a powerful spokesman for the preservation of Constitutional freedoms, for nuclear arms control, and for the protection of the earth's fragile biosphere. The new century with the shock brought about by the 9/11 terror attack was an impetus for him to decry militarization, and his last two works *Timequake* (1997) and his non-fictional *A Man Without a Country* (2005) were manifestations of his sense that "corporate greed, overpopulation, and war would in the end win out over simple humanity". They seem to be a rueful apology to those who would come after him, "We could have saved the world, but we were just too damned lazy." Some newspapers commented on his death in the manner he would probably have liked, using his famous line from *Slaughterhouse-Five:* "So it goes."

[1] Detailed information on the author with special respect to parallels in his autobiography which can be detected in the novel *Slaughterhouse-Five* and compared can be found in ***Copy 8*** *– Who is Kurt Vonnegut, p. 52*

Chronology of Kurt Vonnegut's novels[1]

Player Piano (1952), *The Sirens of Titan* (1959); *Mother Night* (1961), *Cat's Cradle* (1963), *God Bless You, Mr. Rosewater, or Pearls Before Swine* (1965), *Slaughterhouse-Five, or The Children's Crusade: A Duty Dance with Death* (1969), *Breakfast of Champions, or Goodbye Blue Monday* (1973), *Slapstick, or Lonesome no More!* (1976), *Jailbird* (1979), *Deadeye Dick* (1982), *Galápagos: A Novel* (1985), *Bluebird, the Autobiography of Rabo Karabekian* (1916–1988) (1987), *Hocus Pocus* (1990), *Timequake* (1997), *A Man Without a Country, a Memoir of Life in George W. Bush's America* (2005) [essay collection]

The content

Billy Pilgrim, the protagonist, does not live one day after the other. He "has become unstuck in time" which makes it difficult to tell the story. His life is dominated by his six-month experience as a young American soldier in World War II. There he was taken POW by the Germans in the Battle of the Bulge in Luxembourg close to the end of the war in 1944. He survived imprisonment in a former slaughterhouse as well as the bombing of Dresden on 13 February 1945. This core story is not told chronologically, but mottled with clips of different periods of his future life as an optometrist and his kidnapping by aliens, the Tralfamadorians. As a work of fiction, *Slaughterhouse-Five* stands out as extraordinary, due to its combination of autobiographical, historical, sociological, psychological, and science fiction elements in an unprecedented form of montage and collage. Unlike other novels, Vonnegut's novel does not fit a model that stresses plot, character conflict, and climax. The traditional form is dislodged, and Vonnegut offers us a multifaceted, many-dimensional view of fantasy and rock-hard reality.

Chapter overview

Chapter One The author tells the reader about his reasons for writing this "anti-war book" and his struggles in writing it due to his experience as a POW in Dresden when it was bombed. He recalls his meeting with his old war comrade O'Hare and visit back to Dresden in 1967. He introduces Billy Pilgrim as the protagonist of his autobiographical novel.

Chapter Two The most peculiar thing about Billy Pilgrim is that he has become "unstuck in time". This is pointed out in a matter-of-fact way and is supported by the author's characterization: "Billy is spastic in time. He has no control over where he is going next..." He is a time traveller. His travels are described, first from his present to his wedding day in1955 and from then to the war behind German lines in Luxembourg in 1941 and then back to 1963 and we also learn that he had been kidnapped by aliens from Tralfamadore in 1967. He has seen his birth and death several times.
His biography is outlined and his first five time travels all going back to various events in his civilian life are related.

Chapter Three On the battlefield in 1944, Billy and Weary are captured by the Germans. Billy travels in time to his job as an optometrist in 1957 and 1967 in Ilium, N.Y. Back in World War II again, he and other American prisoners are set on a march to get loaded onto railroad cars for transportation from Luxembourg to Germany. Christmas passes while they are in the boxcar. Billy

[1] The long list of short fiction and plays would use a lot of space here.

travels to 1967 and the night he was kidnapped by a flying saucer from Tralfamadore.

Chapter Four On his daughter's wedding night, Billy is kidnapped by the Tralfamadorian aliens. Billy describes the flying saucer. He relates his first philosophical conversation with a Tralfamadorian and, arriving at his alien habitat, a zoo on Tralfamadore, he finds himself back in World War II still in the boxcar. Roland Weary dies of gangrene after he has blamed Billy for his misery. He threatens him to have him killed by an avenger. Billy gets bestowed with a grotesque coat that makes him the clown of the prisoners' troop. He makes two new acquaintances. One of them is Edgar Derby, a high school teacher, who will be shot by the Germans for taking a teapot from the ruins of Dresden as a souvenir. The other one is Paul Lazzaro.
Billy zooms back in time to his infancy, to his job as optometrist, and to his sojourn in the flying saucer.

Chapter Five Billy gives information on the Tralfamadorian view of human beings and their perception of literature. Through a time warp, Billy is flung back into his childhood. At the age of 12, he visits the Grand Canyon and the Carlsbad Caverns with his family. He remembers the holiday as a horror trip.
Back in war, he has to go through delousing. He and the other American POWs are welcomed by singing British POWs who are living comfortably in the internment camp because they were adored by the Germans. Billy falls unconscious and gets a shot of morphine at the hospital. He travels in time to 1948 to Lake Placid, New York, where he is put into a veterans' hospital for non-violent mental patients, three years after the war. There he meets Eliot Rosewater, an infantry captain who introduces Billy to the science fiction works of Kilgore Trout. His mother and his fiancée, Valencia Merble, visit him there. Billy devours the books by K. Trout. He travels in time to the zoo on Tralfamadore where he is displayed and joined by Montana Wildhack. She is brought to him as a mate. Billy learns about the Tralfamadorian way of life and the end of the Universe. He learns about the anti-American propaganda spread by Howard W. Campbell.
He travels to various places in time and finally finds himself home in Ilium in 1968 in his bed scolded by his daughter Barbara who is at a loss, not knowing what to do with him and his claim to have been to Tralfamadore.

Chapter Six Back in 1944, Billy awakens after his morphine night and discovers two lumps in the lining of his coat. Lazzaro reveals himself as Weary's avenger. He threatens Billy to have him killed one day by sending him a killer as he will do with anyone who gets cross with him. He is an eccentric sadist. Billy foresees his own death and when it will occur, 13 February 1976. Swung back to 1945, Billy takes part in the election of E. Derby for their leader. Then they are leaving for Dresden. They arrive at Slaughterhouse Five. (Billy has time travelling experience)

Chapter Seven Five years after his imprisonment in the slaughterhouse, Billy survives an airplane crash he had foreseen in his time travels. In Dresden, the Americans are guarded by a young German, Werner Gluck, when they go to work in a factory producing malt syrup.

Chapter Eight The POWs are visited by Howard W. Campbell, an American who had gone over to the Germans and become a fervent speaker for the German Ministry of Propaganda. He wants to recruit POWs for the German Army against their "common enemy" communism. During his speech, Dresden is bombed. It is the night of 13 February 1945. In his time travel during the Dresden bombardment, he meets Kilgore Trout and invites him to his anniversary party. The bombing of Dresden is conveyed to the reader by Billy telling Montana about it on Tralfamadore.

Chapter Nine After the plane crash, Billy is taken to hospital to have serious brain surgery. When Valencia is informed, she rushes to the hospital, driving like crazy and causing a bad accident on the freeway, losing the exhaust. She has just arrived at the hospital, when she is not able to get out of the car anymore. She dies of suffocation and intoxication. Billy's son Robert, who is doing well as a member of the Green Berets, and his daughter Barbara visit him. His roommate is a Harvard professor of history, Bertram Copeland Rumfoord. The 70-year old historian is working on a book about the Second World War. Rumfoord talks to his twenty-four-year-old wife Lily about the book *The Destruction of Dresden* by David Irving and the dimension of disaster in comparison to Hiroshima. Rumfoord is reluctant to acknowledge Billy's assertion that he had been in Dresden at the time of the bombing. He claims that Billy must suffer from "echolalia".

Billy travels in time to a scene at his optometrist office and to his infancy. He recognizes that his son has changed for the better. In another trip travelling through time, he finds himself on a horse-cart riding through destroyed Dresden looking for souvenirs. In Vermont, Billy escapes from the hospital and goes to New York to tell people about Tralfamadore on the radio.

In a sex shop that Billy mistakes for a library, he finds more Kilgore Trout books and reads about Montana Wildhack.

Chapter Ten The author mentions the recent deaths of Robert Kennedy and Martin Luther King as well as his father's death (1968). Then he gives an account of what he learnt from the Tralfamadorians.

He recollects his trip to East Germany and especially Dresden, during a longer trip through Europe with his friend O'Hare in 1967 (cf. Ch.1). During Billy's trip travelling through time, he is part of a commando gathering the corpses of the air raid and heaping them up in former shelters like the slaughterhouse and incinerating them. He also lost his fatherly friend Edgar Derby. Derby gets arrested for plundering because he has taken a teapot as a war souvenir. The Germans put him to a brief trial and shoot him.

At the end of the war, Billy listens to the birds that are talking, and the last famous sentence reads: "One bird said to Billy Pilgrim, 'Poo-tee-weet?'"

The characters

The author-narrator The author appears himself as a character, mainly in the first and last chapter. His comments and explanations of his experiences as a POW in Dresden at the end of World War II enable the reader to arrive at a more factual interpretation and set the frame for his story about Billy Pilgrim. In the first chapter, he reports on his struggle while writing the book and his final breakthrough thanks to a real person, Mary O'Hare, who reminds him of the war as an insane slaughtering of young boys, who are actually children.

Bernhard V. O'Hare

He is a real-time person and Vonnegut's old war comrade. Vonnegut visits him on behalf of his book project. He and his wife Mary live in Pennsylvania. On the telephone, he is first a little reluctant to reminisce about the war. However, he is a kind host to Vonnegut and provides him with a documentary book on Dresden and other material. Vonnegut and O'Hare like each other and they revisit Dresden together in 1967.

Mary O'Hare

She is a real-time person and Bernard O'Hare's wife. Vonnegut dedicates the book in part to her because she set his mind in the right direction.

Billy Pilgrim

He is the protagonist of the story, a "simple soul", and a classical anti-hero. As an assistant to a chaplain, he survives the Battle of the Bulge and is taken POW behind the German lines. Deported to Dresden, he witnesses the bombardment of the city on 13 February 1945. From then on, he says that he became "unstuck in time". He has no influence on "traveling in time" to different episodes of his life. Private scenes from his marriage and career as an optometrist mix with war scenes and his stay on the planet Tralfamadore.

Roland Weary

He is quite the opposite of Billy Pilgrim. Weary feels utterly fit for the fight; he is a masculine soldier of combat doing his duty in the antitank unit. He is only 18 years old and a cruel pervert and shows that he is worn out by the war. It is the irony of fate that Weary will die because of being captured by the Germans exactly at the moment he wants to kill Billy.

Edgar Derby

He is a caring, well-natured person aged 44 and used to be a teacher. Derby believes in the cause of war and had even volunteered to become a soldier. He is politically interested and courageously speaks his mind in Dresden, when the American Nazi Howard W. Campbell, Jr., holds his recruiting speech in front of the prisoners, expressing contempt for American ideals. But fate has it that this outstanding, decent, and honest man will die a pointless death: he will be sentenced to death by a sudden improvised summary court for alleged plundering. He will take a teapot from the wreckage after the bombing and therefore be shot by a firing squad on the spot.

Paul Lazzaro

He is directly set in contrast to Edgar Derby as "the worst American body". He used to be a car thief from Cicero, Illinois, and is described as Lazarus from the Bible: "he was tiny, and not only were his bones and teeth rotten, but his skin was disgusting. L. was polkadotted all over with dime-sized scars. He had had many plagues of boils". (p. 84) His name is another telling one. He is even more repulsive than Roland Weary, because he really commits sadistic perversities like killing a dog with a spiked steak. He has criminal tendencies and will arrange for Billy's assassination to avenge Weary's death as he has promised him.

Valencia Merble (Billy's wife)

Although Valencia is a fat, plain woman, Billy is satisfied with her as a wife. She really loves him and, as the daughter of Ilium's richest optometrist, she is a real little „dumpling". Her adoration for him is so deep that, when she learns about his plane crash, she hurries to the hospital helter-skelter, wrecking her car on the way. She passes out on her arrival at the hospital and dies in the car because of the carbon monoxide intoxication due to the damaged or lost exhaust pipe. She leaves Barbara and Robert behind, their children.

Tralfamadorians

They are aliens living in a planet too far away to be seen from earth. They will kidnap Billy for "scientific reasons", that is to put him in a kind of zoo on their planet. There they study him in an artificial habitat that offers him everything he needs but no privacy. To watch his sexual behaviour, he is provided with a mate, the lovely film star Montana Wildhack. The Tralfamadorians surround the fish-bowl-like display like curious zoo visitors. Their looks are described as "two feet high, and green, and shaped like plumber's friends", that is toilet plungers, with "a little hand with a green eye in its palm." For them there is no time linearity. They can see in all four dimensions and perceive time as an assemblage of moments that exist simultaneously. They only care for the good moments, and that is the basis of their philosophy. Billy adopts this mindset gladly. It makes him happy and gives peace to his mind. It is their wise equanimity towards the circle of life and the inevitability of death that makes them godlike creatures. Their perspective on life influences the whole structure and narrative style of the novel and finds its prominent expression in the obituary-like "So it goes," whenever the death of someone or something is mentioned.

Montana Wildhack

She is Billy's dream woman: young, pretty, sexy, seductive, and an actress that he first sees and reads about in a sex shop that is camouflaged as an adult bookshop. When Billy is on Tralfamadore, she is brought to him as a mate. She is the one who makes the first shy sexual advances. They have a baby together, and Montana is a loving and caring mother. Billy sees himself and her as the new Adam and Eve in his new Creation of Mankind according to the Tralfamadorian way of conduct.

Howard W. Campbell, Jr.

Billy first comes into contact with his written account of the abhorrent behaviour of American POWs in Germany. Campbell, who seems to be a deserter of the American army, is a dedicated Nazi propagandist trying to recruit men for his Free American Corps to fight the Russians. He speaks in front of the inmates of the slaughterhouse trying to win them over by promising them fine food and a good life. He is a personification of the perversity of war that uses people for mere ideological purposes.

Das Unterrichtsmodell

Vorüberlegungen zum Einsatz des Romans im Unterricht

„Ein literarischer Text, der von Vergangenem erzählt, macht geschichtliche Erfahrungen verfügbar und vermittelt dem Leser die Kenntnis des Gestern als Hilfe zum besseren Verständnis des Heute." So beginnt ein Beitrag von Peter Freese 1977, der Vonneguts Roman *Slaughterhouse-Five* als einen „Glücksfall" für den Englischunterricht betitelt, und er führt die mannigfaltigen Vorzüge des Werkes weiter aus:

„Wenn nun allerdings ein experimenteller Autor, [...], das Konzept des linearen Ablaufs von Zeit aufgibt, Chronologie nicht länger als ‚the straight and uniform string of beads most people think it is' behandelt und postuliert ‚'...(that) we do live our lives simultaneously', dann kann plötzlich ein einziger Text Vergangenheit, Gegenwart und Zukunft gleichermaßen thematisieren und zum Verständnis des Gestern, zur Wahrnehmung des Heute und zum tätigen Einsatz für das Morgen anregen. Kurt Vonneguts Roman ist ein solcher Text: Als ein Roman über die Bombardierung Dresdens, die am 13.2.1945 mit 135 000 Toten nahezu doppelt so viele Opfer forderte wie die Atombombe auf Hiroshima, zwingt *Slaughterhouse-Five* zur Auseinandersetzung mit einem entscheidenden Ereignis der jüngsten Geschichte; als ein Roman über den amerikanischen Alltag der Sechzigerjahre ermöglicht er zahlreiche Einsichten in aktuelle Probleme der Gegenwart, als ein Roman über die Bewohner des Planeten Tralfamadore antizipiert er im Kontrast von irdischen und außerirdischen Lebewesen zukünftige Entwicklungen."[1]

Der Zeitbezug mag heute ein anderer sein und der „Einblick in den Alltag der Sechzigerjahre in Amerika" ist für uns natürlich schon wieder historisch. Dennoch lassen sich die thematischen Aspekte, die der Roman bietet, kaum treffender zusammenfassen. Die große Begeisterung des Didaktikprofessors kann aber nicht über die einzigartige Problematik hinwegtäuschen, die einem das multi-dimensionale und collagenhaft konstruierte Werk für die Umsetzung im Unterricht stellt. Sogar hochmotivierte und leistungsstarke Schülerinnen und Schüler gestanden große Verständnisschwierigkeiten ein, die mit der für sie „verworrenen" Struktur und „unglaubhaften Außerirdischensache" zusammenhingen.

Von einer völlig ungelenkten, spontanen Herangehensweise, bei der die Schülerinnen und Schüler ohne jegliche Vorgabe oder Hilfestellung zum „Alleine lesen" als Vorablektüre animiert werden, ist also abzuraten. Vielmehr muss der Verwirrung von vornherein begegnet werden, indem schon in der *Pre-reading*-Phase auf die zu erwartende Struktur ebenso viel Gewicht gelegt wird wie auf die Inhalte. Man wird zumindest das erste Kapitel intensiv im Unterricht lesen, besser noch die ersten beiden. Danach kann das Buch eigenständig mit einem *Reading Companion* zielgerichtet zu Ende gelesen werden. Eine sinnvolle Beschäftigung mit den literarischen Motiven, historischen und dramatischen Begebenheiten ist nur nach Kenntnis aller Kapitel möglich. [2]

Während der häuslichen Lesephase kann der autobiografische und historische Hintergrund vermittelt werden. Die Besprechung thematischer Schwerpunkte kann durch Hörtextauszüge und Filmausschnitte unterstützt werden.

Der Film sollte nicht vor der Lektüre gesehen werden, denn er weicht inhaltlich etwas ab. Als Abschluss der Einheit ist der Vergleich jedoch reizvoll, gerade wegen der Unterschiede und der genialen Schnitt-Techniken.

---

[1] Freese, Peter, Kurt Vonnegut, Jr., *Slaughterhouse-Five* (1969) in: Der Roman im Englischunterricht der Sekundarstufe II. Paderborn, Schöningh, 1977. Pp. 294–316; p. 294; Freese geht von der damaligen zu hohen Opferzahl aus, die Vonnegut zugrunde legt (A.d.V.).

[2] Vgl. Freese (a.a.O.), p. 298.

Dem Roman wird die Bezeichnung als *science fiction* zwar nicht gerecht, aber Kurt Vonnegut hatte nichts gegen diese Zuordnung. Daher kann die Lektüre an die Thematik *dystopia* anknüpfen. Aus der wahren Absicht des Autors, den Krieg und Amerikas Rolle als Welt(kriegs-)macht zu problematisieren, passt die Lektüre gut in die landeskundliche Einheit *The U.S.A. as a world-power.*

Konzeption des Unterrichtsmodells

Die Einheiten wurden für die Benutzung der Audio-CD[1] konzipiert. Sollte diese nicht verfügbar sein, sind die entsprechenden Passagen zum (Mit-)Lesen ausgewiesen.
Da von einer angeleiteten Vorablektüre des Romans in häuslicher Vorbereitung ausgegangen wird, werden in **Component 1** ausführlich *pre-reading activities* vorgestellt. Die Zeit, die die Schülerinnen und Schüler benötigen, um das Buch nach der gemeinsamen Erarbeitung des ersten Kapitels zur eigenständigen Lektüre und Anlage eines *Reading Companion* zu bewältigen, wird intensiv genutzt. Materialien und Aktivitäten zum historischen Hintergrund sowie z. B. zum Autor schaffen das notwendige Grundlagenwissen zum Verständnis. Das erste Kapitel ist von so entscheidender Bedeutung, dass dieses textintensiv ausgelotet wird. Mit der Hör-CD kann das erste Kapitel inhaltlich in Gruppenarbeit erfasst werden. Das Leitmotiv des „Children's crusade" verdient dabei besondere Beachtung. Das kommunikative Potenzial erhöht sich z. B. durch eine Fragekette zu den Hauptthemen des Romans, wie sie in diesem Kapitel schon angelegt sind.
Sprachlich wird stellvertretend für den gesamten Text der ironische Stil und das „Markenzeichen" des Romans, der legendäre Satz „So it goes" in arbeitsteiliger Gruppenarbeit untersucht. Da Vonneguts Kunst der Verweistechnik für den Roman prägend ist und er eben deswegen so große Beachtung als Literat erlangt hat, sollten die Schülerinnen und Schüler auf die Häufungen von Motiven, Symbolen, Metaphern, etc. aufmerksam werden. Ein Arbeitsblatt, das mit dem *Reading Companion* geführt wird, hilft eine profunde Übersicht zu gewinnen.
Component 2 beschäftigt sich mit dem zentralen Thema des historischen Hintergrundes. Vonneguts Roman ist eine Aufarbeitung seiner Erlebnisse und daher ist ein Vergleich nicht nur unverzichtbar, sondern trägt in hohem Maße zum Verständnis bei. Um ein Einfühlen in die Situation des jungen Soldatens zu ermöglichen, wird mit dem Song „19" gearbeitet und Bilder aus dem Fotoalbum eines Soldaten werden kreativ in einen Tagebucheintrag umgesetzt. Medationsarbeit wird geleistet, wenn ggf. in der Verwandtschaft noch zur Verfügung stehende Zeitzeugen über die Kriegszeit interviewt werden. Dabei hilft ein Wortfeldblatt zum Thema „War and its aftermath". Karten zu Kriegsschauplätzen Ardennen und Dresden veranschaulichen die Schauplätze des Romans. Die Einheit kann als Computer-Projekt gestaltet werden. Dies ist aber nicht zwingend notwendig, dank der vorbereiteten Kopiermaterialien.
In **Component 3** geht es um die Autobiografie Vonneguts, die als Matrize für den Roman dient, und um Billy Pilgrim. Die hohe Übereinstimmung von Vonneguts Erlebnissen mit denen von Billy Pilgrim lässt sich mit dem Textvergleich seiner Biografie und dem Roman gruppenarbeitsteilig leicht in spannende Detektivarbeit verwandeln. Eine ausführliche Biografie, die auf die Textparallelen angelegt ist, wird als Kopievorlage zur Verfügung gestellt. Aus den Strukturfragmenten wird eine lineare Chronologie von Billy Pilgrims Leben herausgedröselt und sorgt für eine Orientierung in der Handlung.
Die folgenden Components wenden sich ganz der Hauptfigur und der Handlung des Romans zu.

[1] Kurt Vonnegut, *Slaughterhouse-Five or the Children's Crusade: A Duty-Dance With Death*, performed by Ethan Hawke, unabridged, includes an interview with the author and an archival author recording set to music. Caedmon, Harper AudioStudios, 2003

Die besondere Struktur, durch die Vonneguts Roman unter anderem literarisch hervorsticht, wird in **Component 4** in einem Gruppenprojekt analysiert und auf „Tapete" gebracht. Ein schauspielerischer Einstieg soll Motivation für die anspruchsvolle Textarbeit schaffen. Billy Pilgrims Zeitreisen bestimmen den Handlungsverlauf. Sie sollen verfolgt und begründet werden. Diese sehr zeitintensive Aktion lässt sich zur Not auch abkürzen. Hierfür können die als Kopiervorlage erarbeiteten Strukturdiagramme kopiert und zur Überprüfung bzw. Kommentierung in Gruppen gegeben werden. Bei der Beschäftigung mit den Zeitreisen kommt der Verdacht auf, dass die Ursache ein Kriegstrauma sein könnte. In einer Pro- und Contra-Debatte kann diese Spekulation lebhaft diskutiert werden. Ein hierzu aufbereiteter Informationstext schafft die nötigen Sachkenntnisse.

Billy Pilgrim erzählt seine Geschichte als Kriegsveteran. Sein Leben lässt sich in drei Phasen fassen: die Erlebnisse im Krieg, als Familienvater und erfolgreicher Optiker, als Prophet der außerirdischen Tralfamadorianer und ihrer „Gelassenheitsphilosophie". Diesen Aspekten tragen die **Components 5** bis **7** insbesondere Rechnung.

In **Component 5** geht es um Billy Pilgrims Kriegserfahrungen. Wie hat er die Zerstörung Dresdens erlebt? Das Schreckliche hat Spuren hinterlassen. Das Trauma erschließt sich in handlungsorientierter, textproduktiver Aktivität. Ein Vergleich mit dem brutalen Roland Weary, der als Standbild inszeniert wird, führt zu einer ethisch-moralischen Betrachtung „soldatischer Tugenden": Was ist Tapferkeit, was ist ein „Held"? Roland Weary muss zu seiner Verhaltensweise auf dem *hot seat* Stellung nehmen.

Die *science fiction*-Komponente des Romans wird in **Component 6** diskutiert. Kann eindeutig beurteilt werden, ob Billy Pilgrim sich die Entführung durch die fliegende Untertasse nur aufgrund seiner Kopfverletzung bei dem Flugzeugabsturz und den Auswirkungen des Kriegstraumas eingebildet hat? Das kann kontrovers debattiert werden. Jedenfalls ist er so sehr von seinem Aufenthalt auf Tralfamadore im „Zoo" zusammen mit seiner Traumfrau Montana Wildhack begeistert, dass er sich am Ende des Romans zum selbsternannten Messias berufen fühlt. Er will die Menschheit mit der Tralfamadorianischen Philosophie beglücken. Dahinter entdecken die Schülerinnen und Schüler die „message" des Autors. Die Funktion der utopischen Episode wird durchschaubar, ebenso wie der formelhafte Satz „So it goes", der die Todesfälle im Roman 104 Mal kommentiert und der von den Tralfamadorianern stammt. Mit Rollenkarten wird eine Talkshow mit Billy, dem Propheten, inszeniert.

Die Gelassenheitsphilosophie der Tralfamadorianer kann musikalisch auf den Punkt gebracht werden und die Interpretation führt zur eigentlichen Absicht des Autors, gegen den Krieg anzuschreiben, wenn es auch so sinnvoll sein mag, wie gegen Gletscher anzuschreiben.

Component 7 führt die inhaltliche Analyse zusammen. Alles zielt auf die eine große Absicht des Autors hin: der Roman soll unmissverständlich ein Anti-Kriegsbuch sein. Die skurrile Struktur, die Anlage des Protagonisten als leicht debilen Schwächling, als Anti-Held *par excellence*, der Stil, der vom Galgenhumor geprägt ist, die philosophischen Gespräche mit den Tralfamadorianern über den freien Willen und Sozialdarwinismus, über Gott und die Welt im wahrsten Sinne des Wortes, alles zielt auf die eine wichtige Botschaft: nie wieder Krieg.

Die Behandlung des Romans kann mit vielerlei multimedial unterstützten handlungsorientierten Aktivitäten abgeschlossen werden. Nicht zuletzt deshalb, weil eine hochkarätige Verfilmung vorliegt und unbedingt herangezogen werden sollte. **Component 8** regt zu *post-reading activities* an. Hier findet sich eine Auswahl an Referat- oder Essaythemen.

Im **Anhang** (*appendix*) befindet sich zum leichteren Umgang mit der Audio-CD parallel zur Buchausgabe ein Verzeichnis der Tracks und entsprechenden Stellen im Buch. Eine Zeittafel informiert über die Rolle der USA im Zweiten Weltkrieg. Die Daten sind im Hinblick auf den Roman ausgewählt.

Für die Leistungsüberprüfung wurden zwei **Klausuren** mit verschiedenem Anspruchsniveau erstellt. **Klausur Nr. 1** (S. 15 ff.) basiert auf einem Sachtext und ist anspruchsvoller als **Klausur Nr. 2** (S. 19 ff.), deren Text dem Roman entnommen ist. Die Aufgaben decken die Bereiche *comprehension, analysis* und *creative text production* ab. Es sind mehrere Aufgaben mit einem Erwartungshorizont zur Auswahl gegeben.

Kurt Vonnegut: Still speaking to the war weary

by Tom Vitale (31 May 2011)

Kurt Vonnegut's blend of anti-war sentiment and satire made him one of the most popular writers of the 1960s, a time when Vietnam dominated the headlines in a way the country's current wars do not. […] the Library of America is republishing four novels written when Vonnegut was at his height of popularity – *Cat's Cradle; God Bless You, Mr. Rosewater; Slaughterhouse-Five* and *Breakfast of Champions*. The central theme in Vonnegut's fiction from the 1960s is the irrationality of governments and the senseless destruction of war. In a 1987 interview, Vonnegut said he was determined to write about war without romanticizing it.

"My own feeling is that civilization ended in World War I, and we're still trying to recover from that," he said. "Much of the blame is the malarkey that artists have created to glorify war which as we all know is nonsense, and a good deal worse than that – romantic pictures of battle, and of the dead and men in uniform and all that. And I did not want to have that story told again."

malarkey *Firlefanz, Blödsinn*

So he approached the subject with humour. His breakthrough to millions of readers came in 1963, with his fourth novel, *Cat's Cradle*, about a secret military experiment, called "Ice Nine" that leads to the destruction of civilization. But his most striking anti-war statement came six years later, and was quickly adapted by Hollywood. *Slaughterhouse-Five* depicts the firebombing of Dresden by Allied warplanes in 1945. […]

The novel is semi-autobiographical. Like its hero, Vonnegut was an American POW, imprisoned in a Dresden slaughterhouse during the air raid. "The destruction of Dresden was my first experience with really fantastic waste", he explained. "To burn down a habitable city and a beautiful one at that… I was simply impressed by the wastefulness, the terrible wastefulness, the meaninglessness of war."

He highlights that meaninglessness by having his main character, Billy Pilgrim, become unstuck in time, reliving random moments of his life – as a young prisoner in Dresden, and as a middle-aged optometrist, captured by aliens for an outer space zoo exhibit.

The story struck a chord with young people facing the draft and a seemingly senseless war in Vietnam. "His reputation was so overwhelming amongst young people", Offit says. "And in a sense, his books were politicized in the culture. They were representative of a point of view that was sweeping the country. Religion is a strong word – but it was almost a religious devotion. And that generates from serious critics who always talked with scepticism: 'Those young people are responding to what? There's nothing complex' – the genius of it was its accessibility."

Offit is a literary critic cited by the author Vidale.

What made them readable in the 1960s makes them readable now, according to Offit – as does their continued relevance.

"There is a serious theme that runs through," Offit explains. "And that theme – that concept of our inhumanity and our self-destruction, and our irrationality – if anything is becoming stronger. God, you read the *Times* in the morning, it seems like Kurt Vonnegut's worst nightmare has come true."

whoopee – super, toll Sache

In a 1991 interview, shortly after the Gulf War, Vonnegut said he was saddened by what he saw in America. "We have become such a pitiless people", Vonnegut lamented. "And I think it's TV that's done it to us. When I went to war in World War II, we had two fears. One was we would be killed. The other was that we might have to kill somebody. And now killing is Whoopee. It does not seem much anymore. To my generation, it still seemed like an extraordinary thing to do, to kill." (653 words)

The Gulf War (2 August 1990 – 28 February 1991), codenamed *Operation Desert Storm* (17 January 1991 – 28 February 1991) was a war waged by a UN-authorized coalition force led by the United States against Iraq in response to Iraq's invasion and annexation of Kuwait.

Tom Vitale: Kurt Vonnegut: Still speaking to the war weary (shortened).
URL: http://www.npr.org/2011/05/31/136823289/kurt-vonnegut-still-speaking-to-the-war-weary (Aufruf: 4.7.2013)

Assignments

Comprehension

1. Summarize Vonnegut's literary intention and use of a different approach of conveying it as laid out in the text.

2. Why did *Slaughterhouse-Five* strike a chord with young people? Refer to the text and state your own opinion.

Analysis

3. Explain Offit's cry of horror: "God, you read the *Times*[1] in the morning, it seems like Kurt Vonnegut's worst nightmare has come true." Go beyond the text.

4. "We have become such a pitiless people." Comment on Vonnegut's deep sigh by referring to the text. Support his opinion by giving an example from the novel *Slaughterhouse-Five.*

Creative writing

5. What will become of Montana Wildhack? Imagine Montana Wildhack sitting in the cage in the Tralfamadorian zoo. She is writing a report on her life there with Billy for presenting it to the media in case she might be able to return to the Earth one day. Write that report.

---

[1] ***The Times*** is a moderate, sometimes conservative daily national newspaper. It has been published in Britain since 1785 and in America, since 2006.

Erwartungshorizont zu Klausur 1

Zu 1:
- He wants to show the "irrationality of governments and the senseless destruction of war".
- "He was determined to write about war without romanticizing it."
- He accuses writers who wrote glorifying unrealistic novels about war of seducing young, easily influenced people into it by drawing a romantic picture of the battle and the hero in a shiny uniform as if it was a game; he did not want to write another piece in that romantic fairy-tale style.
- So he needed a new approach and found it using a different style and humour, even black humour.
- He also added fantastic and science fiction elements to his novels e.g. the idea of the destruction of all civilization in *Cat's Cradle* or the idea of becoming "unstuck in time" as in *Slaughterhouse-Five.*

Zu 2: The novel was released when a lot of young men were drafted for the war against Vietnam:
- "His books were politicized in the culture."
- They were representative of a point of view that was sweeping the country. Religion is a strong word – but it was almost a religious devotion. As serious critics who always talked with scepticism stated:
- " 'There's nothing complex' – the genius of it was its accessibility."
- "There is a serious theme that runs through", Offit explains. "And that theme – that concept of our inhumanity and our self-destruction, and our irrationality – if anything is becoming stronger."

Own opinion: individual answers based on the lecture and lessons about the novel are expected.

Zu 3: Reading *The Times* is a symbol for becoming a mainstream personality. Vonnegut dreaded the saturated middle class. In the novel, he uses the metaphor of the glasses; people cared more for the frames of the glasses than for the glasses. They do not care about seeing clearly but they care instead about their appearances. The preference of appearance to reality and genuine values is a mark of these ignorant people who do not want to see the truth. The truth or reality confronts them with the bad, the ugly, the inhumane side of life, uncomfortable circumstances, and finally with themselves and death. Adapting to bourgeois patterns means giving in to the mechanisms of mediocrity and manipulation from those ruling above. Vonnegut's nightmare was that people lose their critical minds by accepting what this type of conservative newspaper, for example, prescribes. Such newspapers are instruments that influence people so that they remain at a stage of knowledge very much like that of Billy Pilgrim, the naïve patriotic citizen at the mercy of some unfathomable leaders and their commands.

Zu 4: Point of discussion: Vonnegut refers to America's active participation in another war. The operation "Desert Storm" was broadcast live on television. The whole world could watch the real-time nightly bombardment in flickering green and black pictures from a special night sight camera. The broadcast was a matter of discussion in itself. Vonnegut's guess was right: like Billy Pilgrim, martial patriotic mindsets have not been sobered or reached by the massacres already witnessed and survived in the previous world wars. It doesn't end. As he expressed it, he might as well have written an "anti-glacier" book. How effective has it been, if people still go out slaughtering with heavy weapons, with no regard for losses? In the novel, Billy Pilgrim does not really blame or accuse anyone of the killing, but he testifies to the cruelty and barbaric act of the bombing of Dresden that not only killed some German guards, but also their families, to which they returned that day, happy in the security that Dresden was absolutely secure since there was no military interest in destroying it. Children were killed, as for e.g. those refugee girls, Billy, his comrades and Werner Gluck, that young German soldier, encountered by accident when they were undressing in a neighbouring slaughterhouse. But Billy could also have easily been killed by his own folks: a lot of people searching shelter in the basements of houses or, as Billy, in the underground meat locker were buried alive or suffocated there by the smoke of the fires everywhere. Other Allied prisoners of war died because of the aftermath of the raid. The corpses had to be heaped up and burnt by POWs like the Maori prisoner doing forced traumatic work. They were killed or suffered lifelong trauma. If people have pity, they cannot wage war against any nation in an age matured by enlightenment and at a peak of scientific and technical progress, capable of blowing the whole globe to pieces. Humankind should be able to handle all conflicts with common sense and in the name of peace.

Zu 5:

- Information on the planet and the Tralfamadorians (physics and philosophy).
- Her abduction and awakening naked in the presence of Billy Pilgrim.
- How and why she fell in love with him.
- What Billy told her about the war.
- How she feels about him.
- How she feels about herself as someone who has been torn out of a career in show business.
- Will people on earth remember her?
- The raising of the child in that isolated place worries her.
- Will they ever return?
- What would life be like if they returned?
- What about Billy's family?
- Wishes, hopes, dreams, fears …

serve. The Club serves his business purposes only. Meeting influential, prospective business partners is all he wants. It is a matter of prestige and not of real humanitarian charity.
As a veteran, he has become rich and concentrates on his job and family. He does not care about the subject of war anymore. He does not even care for the conservation of his past. The tearing down of his old birthplace doesn't matter to him. The fact that he agrees with "urban renewal" is another indication for his attitude towards everything: "so it goes". Billy cannot change anything after all, and why should he, since everything is already determined, as he knows from the Tralfamadorians.

Zu 4: After treatment in a veteran's hospital, he feels quite well. He manages to finish his studies and gets married. With his wife Valencia, he has two children, Robert and Barbara. He becomes a rich optometrist who is good at his job. At least as long as he does not have the feeling that something is wrong. He falls asleep during his work and jumps in time. Then, on the night of his daughter's wedding day, he is kidnapped by the Tralfamadorian saucer. At least, this is what he tells people and the whole country, via letters to the newspapers and even the radio. People consider him ill and demented from then on. They conclude that he suffers from post-war trauma and the effects of the plane crash. There he had suffered severe damage to the brain. So the lookers-on think that Billy Pilgrim starts imagining the "time-travels" and encounter with Montana Wildhack on Tralfamadore as a reaction to this physiological and psychological condition. The idea of the kidnapping and being naked with an attractive female mate occurs to Billy Pilgrim after the tragic car accident which happened to his beloved wife Valencia. This also supports the medical indication with regard to his stress fantasies.

Zu 5: Individual answers are expected. References to his first impression of "OZ", memories of the time there as a POW, some pondering about the time under Honecker and the reconstruction [simply mentioning this would be fine – detailed knowledge is not expected], the absurdity and futility of first destroying the city and then re-building it and living there as if nothing had ever happened. A positive conclusion: everything is well again, and perhaps people will learn the lesson of avoiding another war through the ruins and reconstruction…

Component 1

Creating expectations and setting the frame

Der Roman *Slaughterhouse-Five* ist für Schülerinnen und Schüler wegen seiner Struktur problematisch. Weniger Probleme bereiten die Sprache und der handliche Umfang. Die Thematik des Zweiten Weltkrieges liegt außerhalb des Erfahrungsbereiches der Schülerinnen und Schüler. Vorkenntnisse aus dem Geschichtsunterricht sind wünschenswert.
Das Identifikationspotenzial für die Schülerinnen und Schüler mit dem Antihelden Billy Pilgrim ist in Bezug auf seine äußere Erscheinung eher gering. Seine Person wird jedoch reizvoll dadurch, dass er ein flapsiger junger Mann ist, der mit zwanzig in den Krieg zieht und eigenartige Zeitsprünge erlebt. Der Roman lebt von dieser Eigenschaft und hat einen „experimentellen" Charakter, der die Spannung zum Weiterlesen schafft. Die *Pre-reading*-Phase dient zum einen dazu, zur Lektüre positiv zu motivieren, Hintergrundwissen zu aktivieren oder zu liefern, Hilfestellung für das Verständnis der komplizierten Struktur zu geben, und zum anderen, den Zeitraum, den die angeleitete Vorablektüre in häuslicher Vorbereitung in Anspruch nimmt, inhaltlich optimal zu gestalten.

1.1 Getting started

Die Schülerinnen und Schüler sollen mittels einer kreativen *quick writing activity* mit der historischen Thematik des Romans bekannt gemacht werden. Sie erhalten den Auftrag, einen Stift und ein Papier zur Hand zu nehmen und ohne abzusetzen zu schreiben, nachdem sie das Bild, das gleich auf dem Projektor gezeigt werden wird, gesehen haben. Sie sollen erst anhalten, wenn ein „Stopp"-Zeichen gegeben wird. Arbeitsanweisungsfolge:

1. Take a pen and a piece of paper.
2. Do not speak with your partner anymore. This has to be done individually and silently.
3. Look at the picture and start writing immediately. You can write sentences, words, or phrases, but do not stop writing.
4. Let your mind flow regarding what you see and what comes into your mind.
5. Stop writing when I tell you to.

Die Darstellung der Frauenkirche von Dresden (*Getting Started*, S. 3) wird nun eingeblendet. Kopieren Sie so, dass auf der Folie eine Beschriftung möglich ist (s. S. 23) oder projizieren Sie so, dass Sie die Tafel parallel benutzen können.
Die Schreibphase kann 3 bis 5 Minuten währen. Danach werden Ideen, die bei dem *brainstorming* entstanden sind, locker abgefragt. Es ist nicht notwendig, dass die Schülerinnen und Schüler ihre Aufschriebe wortgetreu vorlesen. Sollte jedoch das Bedürfnis bei einigen bestehen, kann dies gewährt werden. Wichtige Effekte der Aktion ist, dass die Schülerinnen und Schüler untereinander ihre verschiedenen Sichtweisen wahrnehmen und dass sich schon herausstellt, ob konkretes Wissen über Dresden und die Kriegszerstörung da ist. Viel-

leicht erkennen die Schülerinnen und Schüler das Gebäude der Frauenkirche, dies wird jedoch nicht erwartet.
Die Aufmerksamkeit wird hiernach nochmals auf das Bild als solches gelenkt; im fragend-entwickelnden Gespräch können folgende Bezüge zur Lektüre hergestellt werden, die auf der Folie notiert werden.
Leitfragen und mögliche Antworten je nach historischem Kenntnisstand der Klasse:

1. How is this picture made?

   This is a collage showing a montage of three pictures of the "Church of Our Lady" in Dresden.

2. What do the three pictures signify?

   Each shows a different stage of the building: the first one shows the church before the war, the second, the war ruin, and finally, there is a picture of the rebuilt church.

3. What does this trio tell us symbolically?

   It shows the pointlessness of war and destruction, the insanity of war, the waste of resources, energies, cultural achievements, lives; it symbolizes the destruction caused by the American air raid in 1945.

The Church of Our Lady

Montage of three pictures: 1. before the war 2. war ruin 3. reconstruction	= technique of the novel
a symbol of the destruction of Dresden on February 13, 1945 by heavy firebombing	= autobiographical /historical central topic of the novel
The message to us is: war is pointless, insane destruction and it must never happen again!	= the book is an anti-war novel with exactly this message

Jetzt können die Bücher ausgeteilt, oder falls schon geschehen, herangezogen werden.

1.2 Three titles – creating expectations

Schon die allererste Seite ist eine Überraschung. Das Buch hat einen Titel und zwei weitere. Kurt Vonnegut sah alle drei gleichberechtigt und tatsächlich spiegeln sie die drei wichtigen Themenkomplexe des Romans wider: Die Kriegsgefangenschaft als solche im Dresdner Schlachthof, die Tatsache, dass viele der Soldaten noch halbe Kinder waren, und die Absurdität des Krieges mit seinen sinnlosen Toten. Die Schülerinnen und Schüler sollen nun intuitiv in Assoziation mit der vorangegangenen Heranführung an die Dresden-Thematik ihre

Erwartungen in Verbindung mit den Titeln im Klassengespräch äußern. Je nachdem, wie viele Informationen man schon über das Buch im Vorfeld gegeben hat, werden die Ergebnisse variieren. Diese werden an der Tafel festgehalten und können z. B. nach Abschluss der Lektüre verifiziert werden. Mögliches Resultat an der Tafel:

Kurt Vonnegut (1969)

Slaughterhouse-Five

⇩

- a place where animals are killed to produce food
- Do people perhaps get killed there by a mad murderer?
- a special slaughterhouse because of the number "5"; are there more?
- …

or The Children's Crusade:

⇩

- a historical event concerning children
- crusade: crusaders fought against Muslims for the Christian faith.
- In 1215 …
- religious fanaticism
- …

A Duty-Dance with Death

⇩

- duty–dance: this is a strange combination as a dance is something voluntarily done. If it is duty, it is forced upon you and a burden rather than a treat.
- with death: death as a person (allegory) dances with you. That's irony or sarcasm.
- going round in circles with death → inevitability of death, circle of life, omni-presence of death everywhere, irrelevance of death in the course of time

Nun kann der restliche Text der ersten Seite laut gelesen werden. Es sollte den Schülerinnen und Schülern als ungewöhnlich auffallen, dass ein Autor eine so umfangreiche und selbstironische biografische Aussage vor seinen eigentlichen Text stellt. Die Schülerinnen und Schüler geben in eigenen Worten wieder, was Vonnegut über sich und sein Buch aussagt. Das „Selbstporträt" ist ein eindeutiger Hinweis darauf, dass es sich um einen stark autobiografischen Roman handeln wird, in dem Vonnegut seine Erfahrungen als POW verarbeitet. Zum ersten Mal wird die konkrete Situation der Bombardierung Dresdens erwähnt. Wichtig ist die Erklärung der Methode als „telegraphic schizophrenic manner of tales of the planet Tralfamadore". Dies bereitet auf die eigenartige *stream of consciousness*-Struktur und zu erwartenden *science fiction*-Elemente vor. Das am Ende lapidar gesetzte „peace" weist Vonnegut der amerikanischen Friedensbewegung zu und ist Ausdruck seines literarischen und ideologischen Anliegens.

Damit ist der thematische Rahmen gesetzt. Lassen Sie die Schülerinnen und Schüler über den Zweck historischer Dichtung diskutieren. Liefert sie nur einen illustren Hintergrund für eine Geschichte, oder spielt es eine Rolle, wann eine Geschichte stattfindet? Was kann man vom Lesen einer Geschichte, die in einer anderen als der eigenen geschichtlichen Periode angesiedelt ist, lernen?

This book is a piece of historical fiction. With reference to your own reading experience, does history just provide a colourful background for a story, or does it matter to a story when it takes place? What can you learn from reading a story that is set in a different historical period from your own?

Wenn man den historischen Hintergrund durch SchülerInnenbeiträge in Form von Kurzreferaten gestalten oder auflockern möchte, dann können jetzt die Themen wie z. B. „Dresden", „the American involvement in World War II", „Kurt Vonnegut" , „The Children's crusade", „Death-dance imagery in literature and the arts", etc. vergeben werden. Für die Erarbeitung der Daten und Fakten kann alternativ oder ergänzend eine auf einem Arbeitsblatt basierende computergestützte Recherche nach der gemeinsamen Lektüre des ersten Kapitels angestellt werden. (Siehe Component 2: Der historische und autobiografische Hintergrund, ***Copy 6, The war locations,*** S. 45)

1.3 The metafictional frame in chapter one – the preface

Das erste Kapitel soll ganz gelesen und bearbeitet werden. Der Textanfang kann von CD[1] eingespielt werden (T1 [0:00–0:57])
Der berühmte amerikanische Schauspieler, Ethan Hawke, liest auf der CD auch die erste Seite, die bereits bearbeitet wurde, die Widmung und das Gedicht. Diese kurzen Teile (1 min) werden zunächst gespielt oder gelesen und mit zwei „Beobachtungaufträgen" bedacht. Über die Bedeutung des Gedichts können die Schülerinnen und Schüler spekulieren. Dazu kann es sinngemäß übersetzt werden:
Das Rind muht/ Das Kind erwacht/ Aber der kleine Herr Jesus /Kein Geschrei macht.

1. Let's see if we find out later on why the book is dedicated to Mary O'Hare and Gerhard Müller.
2. Can you make anything of this little poem?
3. Why do you think did Vonnegut put these lines at the beginning?

Die Schülerinnen und Schüler werden spekulieren, dass es im Roman vielleicht um ein Kind gehen wird, dass es irgendwie um Religion gehen könnte. Nahe an der Bedeutung läge eine Vermutung in die Richtung, dass das Gedicht auf die Hauptperson gemünzt sein könnte, die wie ein unschuldiges Kind durch etwas gestört wird, aber mit nahezu übermenschlicher Geduld alles, was da kommt, erträgt. Dies wird jedoch nicht erwartet. Die Spekulation soll unkommentiert stehen bleiben. Es wird lediglich darauf hingewiesen, dass man das Gedicht nicht vergessen soll, denn der Autor hat die vier Zeilen gewiss mit Absicht an den Anfang gestellt.

1.4 Vorablektüre mit dem *Reading Companion*

Der Lerngruppe wird ein Langzeit-Leseauftrag erteilt. Das Buch soll von nun an selbstständig bis zu einem festzulegenden Datum (ca. zwei Wochen) ganz gelesen werden.
Die Zeit im Unterricht dient der Erarbeitung des historischen und autobiografischen Hintergrundes. Hier finden beispielsweise Schülerpräsentationen, Filmdokumente und Internet-Recherche ihren Platz.
Der Leseprozess soll von einem *Reading Companion* begleitet werden. Die verwirrende Struktur des Buches macht dieses Notizbuch sehr wertvoll. Dokumentiert werden sollen vor allem die Zeitsprünge, die Billy Pilgrim erlebt. Hilfreich für die Orientierung wird die Anweisung sein, für die in Erscheinung tretenden Personen je eine Farbe zum Unterstreichen im Buch festzulegen. Der *Reading Companion* kann so aufgebaut sein (DIN A 4 Querformat):

---

[1] Kurt Vonnegut, *Slaughterhouse-Five or the Children's Crusade*: A Duty Dance with Death. Performed by Ethan Hawke, unabridged, Caedmon, Harper Audio, 2003

Chapter/page	Person(s)	Plot	Notes/Questions
1 pp. ? -?	The author-narrator; Mary and Bernard V. O'Hare (Indirect: Edgar Derby)	The narrator mentions his problems in writing his "anti-war novel"; we learn about the autobiographical and historical background and special structure of the book.	Setting: USA 1967 Topics: World War II; Dresden; Battle of the Bulge; Children's Crusade

Im Laufe des Unterrichts kommen weitere Aufträge dazu, z. B. auf das Auftauchen des Begriffs „Children's Crusade", auf Altersangaben, die Zeitsprünge, Symbole und ironische Textpassagen zu achten.

1.5 Erarbeitung des *prologue*

Die Lektüre des ersten Kapitels kann nun in Sequenzen beginnen. Die Lese-/Hörphase dient zunächst der Erfassung des Inhalts. In einer anschließenden Phase beschäftigen sich die Schülerinnen und Schüler intensiver mit dem Text, der die grundlegenden Aussagen zur literarischen Technik und den Themen bildet.

1. Hör-/Lese-Sequenz (HLS):

Die Schülerinnen und Schüler lesen zur CD ca. 7 Minuten lang still mit (T1[0:57 – 7:24]; bis p. 5 „That's your trade not mine"). Nach der Klärung des Vokabulars soll der erste Leseeindruck auf den offenen Impuls hin geäußert werden:

What is your impression of what you have just read and heard?

Die individuellen Eindrücke werden sich auf den Autor und dessen selbst-ironische ("I have become an old fart....", p. 2) und leicht anstößige Ausdrucksweise beziehen. Der schlüpfrige Limerick dürfte ebenso rätselhaft sein, wie das „Endloslied" „My name is Yon Yonson"[1]. Hier begegnet man schon der„zusammengeklebten" sprunghaft-assoziativen Eigenart des Textes.
Die Schülerinnen und Schüler werden merken, dass Vonnegut sich eigentlich wiederholt. Er hat ja schon in dem „Vorwort" auf den historischen Hintergrund der Geschichte hingewiesen, hier führt er dies in Einzelheiten aus. Er spricht über die Schwierigkeiten, die er mit der Anfertigung des Anti-Kriegsromans hatte, und seine Rückkehr nach Dresden 1967.
Auffallen sollte auch, dass es sich um keine reine Autobiografie handeln wird. Es heißt im ersten Satz: "All this happened more or less."

[1] Yon Yonson: Den *Lumberjack Song* sowie den Limerick hat Vonnegut nicht selbst erfunden. „Yon Yonson" ist in Amerika als Endlosreim ca. seit 1899 durch schwedische Einwanderer bekannt. Siehe http://www.vanishedamericana.com/old-time-fun/yon-yonson-1899-stage-play-poster/ (Aufruf: 4.2.2013)

Bevor die zweite Sequenz gelesen wird, lässt sich schon die Frage nach der Widmung für Gerhard Müller beantworten:

> Haven't we come across a certain Gerhard Müller before?
>
> Gerhard Müller is one of the people the book is dedicated to. Vonnegut appreciates very much that he bore no grudge against the Americans who were responsible for the death of his mother. She lost her life in the incineration of Dresden. Despite his terrible experiences, he had sent a Christmas peace card of hope and conciliation.

2. Hör-/Lese-Sequenz :

Der erste *Track* wird zu Ende gespielt [T1(7:24–12:20)]. Es wird bis p. 8 ("...things I learned in college after the war.") mitgelesen. Auf die eigentümliche Arbeitsweise mit der Tapete wird noch explizit und „haptisch" zurückgegriffen.
Zunächst sollen die Schülerinnen und Schüler die biografischen Informationen des *author-narrator* in Partnerarbeit stichwortartig aus dem Text filtern. Diese Sammlung wird im weiteren Verlauf noch ergänzt, daher sollte ein Hinweis auf eine Platzaussparung gegeben werden. Am besten legt man ein gesondertes Blatt an. Die Zusammenstellung wird später zu einem weiteren Vergleich mit einerseits den tatsächlichen autobiographischen Daten Vonneguts, dem Erzähler und seiner Figur Billy Pilgrim herangezogen (vgl. S. 47). Für die spätere Kontrollbesprechung kann einem Paar eine Folie gegeben werden. Es stellt dann seine Ergebnisse am Overhead-Projektor vor, z. B.:

Biographical information provided by the author-narrator (Chapter 1):

- The war parts of the story are fairly true. (p. 1)
- One person he knew was shot in Dresden for taking a teapot. (p. 1)
- Another person threatened to have his personal enemies killed by hired gunmen after the war. (p. 1)
- He changed the names. (p. 1)
- He went back to Dresden in 1967 with old war companion Bernard V. O' Hare. (p. 1)
- He made friends with cab driver Gerhard Müller who had been a prisoner of war of the Americans. (p. 2)
- Writing books costs a lot of money and time. (p. 2)
- He has full grown sons (p. 2) = babies (p. 7).
- He turns the project of writing the book around in his mind for a long time. (p. 2–3)
- He lived on Cape Cod. (p. 3)
- He wants his old war companion Bernard V. O'Hare to help him. They had been privates in the war: infantry scouts. (p. 4)
- As a POW he had been freed by a POW exchange a couple of weeks after the war ended, near Halle. (p. 5–6)
- He had taken a Luftwaffe saber as souvenir. (p. 6)
- He was nursed in a rest camp at France to put on "baby fat". (p. 7)
- He married a pretty girl at home who was covered with "baby fat". (p. 7)
- He has a dog called Sandy. He likes her very much as a talking partner. (p. 7)
- He went to study at the University of Chicago after WWII and was a student in the Department of Anthropology. (p. 8)

(continued... after HLS 3:)

- During his studies he had worked as a newspaper reporter for the famous Chicago City News Bureau. (p. 8)

- Later he became a public relations man for General Electric in Schenectady, New York, and a volunteer fireman in the village of Alplaus where he settles down. (p. 10)
- Those were financially hard times, the "scrawny years". (p. 10–11)
- He and his wife have a lot of veteran friends. (p. 11)
- His letter to the Air Force asking them for details about the raid on Dresden is answered with the warning that the information was still top secret. (p. 11)
- He visits Bernhard O'Hare in 1964. (p. 11)
- At O'Hare's house he remembers two Russians who had looted a clock factory and used a horse wagon to carry away their prey. (p. 14)

(continued... after HLS 4:)

- The narrator worked as a teacher of creative writing in the famous Writers Workshop at the University of Iowa while he was working on the novel. (p. 18)
- He received a three-book contract by Seymour Lawrence. (p. 18)
- He told his sons never to become soldiers or engage in any business that can cause massacre. (p. 19)
- He revisited Dresden with O'Hare. (p. 19)

Die Schülerinnen und Schüler sollen überlegen, warum es Vonnegut wohl solch ein Bedürfnis ist, so ausführlich von seinen Schwierigkeiten mit dem Buch zu schreiben. (vgl. p. 2 "I would hate to tell you what this lousy little book cost me ...") Ist das interessant oder eher frustrierend? O'Hare und Edgar Derby scheinen tragende Funktionen in der Geschichte zu haben, was vermuten die Schülerinnen und Schüler?

1. Why does Vonnegut tell us so much about why he wrote the book and how difficult it was?

   References to the text with a focus on his assertion that there is no real way to write about a massacre are expected.

2. Is it interesting, or is it frustrating to have to read about this before starting the story? Why would Vonnegut feel it necessary to start the book in this manner?

   Individual answers are expected.

3. Make a guess as to why O'Hare was first "unenthusiastic" to assist Vonnegut with his memories of the war.

   He wants to forget about the past, unpleasant memories, nightmare; recalling means living through it again...

4. What role could be bestowed on Edgar Derby and why?

   Students can guess that he must be the hero of the story, but he will not be the main character, as will be learnt later on.

Zur Vervollständigung der Sammlung biografischer Daten aus der dritten Hörsequenz (p. 8 bis p. 15 "She was my friend after that.") können die Schülerinnen und Schüler diese in häuslicher Vorbereitung lesen und entsprechend auswerten. (Siehe Tafelbild oben, ab „continued", Einträge ab p. 8).

Die folgende Stunde beginnt mit den biografischen Ergänzungen, danach folgt die

3. Hör-/Lese-Sequenz:

Track 2 (11:31 min) wird ununterbrochen gespielt. Er endet auf p. 15 ("...She was my friend after that."). Direkt nach dem Anhören kann die Widmung an Mary O'Hare erklärt werden:

> The book is also dedicated to Mary O'Hare. Why?
>
> At first, Mary O'Hare is annoyed about the narrator's visit. She thinks that he is going to write another glorification of war as a "test-field" for the strongest and bravest supermen shooting down their enemies in the cowboy style of John Wayne. But only when the narrator solemnly swears that he will not write this type of action thriller but an anti-war novel does she consent to help him with his research and becomes his friend. She is the one who makes the allusion to the children's crusade by pointing out that the narrator and her husband had just been "babes" that went to war. So the book owes its second title to her.

Auf die Geschichte mit dem Aufzugführer wird unter dem Aspekt der Ironie zurückgekommen. Hier wird sie zunächst ausgespart, um zügig zum Ende des Kapitels zu kommen.
Vor der Einspielung und dem Lesen der letzten Kapitelpassage erhalten die Schülerinnen und Schüler den Hörauftrag, weitere biografische Informationen zu markieren:

> Underline further biographical information.

4. Hör-/Lese-Sequenz:

Track 3 (11:43) wird präsentiert. Die Schülerinnen und Schüler erfahren hier konkret, weshalb einer der Titel des Buches „The Children's Crusade" heißt.
Zuerst wird im Unterrichtsgespräch eine Auswertung des Hörauftrages vorgenommen. Die biografischen Informationen, die unterstrichen wurden, werden der Sammlung (siehe oben) zugefügt.
Das Kapitel schließt mit dem Anfang des zweiten Kapitels ab und führt so recht unvermittelt die Hauptperson, Billy Pilgrim, ein. Die Schülerinnen und Schüler sollen bei ihrer häuslichen Lektüre darauf achten, inwiefern der Erzähler dieser Gestalt seine biografischen Züge verliehen hat. Die Parallelen sollen in den *Reading Companions* besonders vermerkt werden, sodass sie zum Vergleich, später auch mit den autobiografischen Daten Vonneguts, schnell gefunden werden können. (Siehe 3.1. Who is Kurt Vonnegut?)

1.6 *The Children's Crusade* (Exkurs zum Leitmotiv)

Die historischen Fakten zum Kinderkreuzzug und der ersten großen Zerstörung Dresdens, die Vonnegut zitiert[1], stimmen, sodass an dieser Stelle zunächst eine Zusammenfassung zur Klärung des Textverständnisses ausreichen kann.
Da der Kinderkreuzzug aber erfahrungsgemäß eine große Faszination bei Schülerinnen und Schüler auslöst und Leitmotiv des Romans ist, lohnt sich hier ein vertiefender Exkurs.
Es wird nicht erwartet, dass die Schülerinnen und Schüler vom Kinderkreuzzug wissen. Die Tatsache, dass Vonnegut das historische Himmelfahrtskommando als einen seiner Titel gewählt hat und hier sogar mit großem Textzitat ausführt, soll den Schülerinnen und Schülern

[1] Beide Werke, Mackays *Extraordinary Popular Delusions and the Madness of Crowds*, sowie Mary Endells *Dresden, History Stage and Gallery* sind reale Monografien. Beide sind noch im Handel. Mackay erfuhr mehrere Nachdrucke und ist als *e-book* erhältlich. Endell wurde repliziert durch *Book on Demand.*

verdeutlichen, dass es sich hier um ein Leitmotiv handelt. Hier lässt sich auch das bereits erwähnte Eingangsgedicht heranziehen, um die Bedeutung zu veranschaulichen: Es wurden – wieder – Kinder in den Krieg geschickt und wissentlich in den Tod.

Es bietet sich an, nun eine im Voraus zum Thema vergebene Präsentation abhalten zu lassen oder einen Film, z. B. „Kreuzzug der Kinder"[1] heranzuziehen. Dieser macht die Umstände der religiös-fanatischen Mission verständlich. Da die Filmsprache Deutsch ist, kann sich an das gemeinsame Sehen eine einfache Mediationsübung anschließen, in der je zwei Schülerinnen und Schüler miteinander die gesehenen Informationen auf Englisch schriftlich sammeln und anschließend einen Reisetagebucheintrag oder einen Brief in der Rolle eines erwachsenen Mitfahrers verfassen:

Let's pretend you took part in the Crusade as an accompanying priest. Describe the journey in your travel journal or in a letter home either to your family or to the pope.

Points of interest:
Fanatic leader, charismatic spell, terrifying threat of being doomed to hell if one did not obey orders, hardship, starvation, sore feet, begging for food, illness, sent back by good people, agony on the ship, dying children all around...

Die leitmotivische Bedeutung des "Children's crusade" lässt sich am gesamten Romantext belegen. Dazu erhalten die Schülerinnen und Schüler den Auftrag, Passagen, in denen entweder wieder von dem Kinderkreuzzug gesprochen wird, oder es um das Alter der Personen geht, im *Reading Companion* gut zu dokumentieren.

Nachdem das erste Kapitel nun bekannt ist, kann seine Funktion in Partnerarbeit oder als Hausaufgabe schriftlich erfasst werden.

What is this first chapter about? Write down the main issues and what strikes you as most odd for an introduction to a novel. Form some questions to ask your classmates.

Main issues:
The narrator is very present and talks about his difficulties in writing the novel. He tells the readers that he had been a POW and survived the incineration of Dresden. He revisited Dresden in 1967 and did research for the book with the help of his wartime companion Bernard O' Hare. He says that he is definitely going to write an anti-war book as he has promised this to Mary O'Hare who compares WWII to the historical Children's Crusade.

Odd features:
The introduction is not a direct introduction to the story of the novel. Only at the very end does he mention Billy Pilgrim, but even this is not a usual way of presenting the main protagonist, the setting, and so forth. Two characters are merely mentioned, Edgar Derby and Lazzaro. But nothing more is said about them. One could guess that Derby is the hero of the story, but he isn't.
There is nothing about the aliens as one might have expected from the preface-like inscription at the very beginning of the book. The first chapter is more like an account of the writing process and the issues and topics dealt with.

[1] Terra X Vol.10, Der Kreuzzug der Kinder u.a., Universum GmbH, frei ab 12, ersch. Nov. 2009

It also functions as an apology. The narrator apologizes several times for the book being a failure. His apology to his editor and the readers for the confused structure of the novel reads: "It is so short and jumbled and jangled, Sam, because there is nothing intelligent to say about a massacre." (p. 19) Such a statement is very uncommon in a literary introduction.
Furthermore, it strikes one as odd that the narrator presents long passages of secondary literature on the historical facts of the Children's Crusade and the first destruction of Dresden. He even cites Goethe in German. (p. 15–18) He must have felt the need of creating a strong basis for what he was going to do. He therefore creates a very realistic metafictional frame around the novel.
This is important because the structure of this chapter already indicates that the narrative line will probably run out of chronology. There is the interpolation of the limerick, for example, that at first irritates the reader but then, when reading is continued, you recognize that something like free association is being used.

Possible student questions:
So the narrator himself seems quite odd. How else can one account for his distorted perception of time when he recalls the Lufthansa delay situation? (p. 20) Why does he refer to himself as an "Earthling" if he is not at least slightly mad? Why does he call himself "an old fart" so disparagingly at least twice on the first pages of his book? Why does he say that there is no adequate form for writing about massacre? Why does he so explicitly point out the warning of his sons not to take part in anything that has to do with massacre?

Nach der gemeinsamen Besprechung der schriftlichen Aufgaben stellen sich die Schülerinnen und Schüler gegenseitig ihre Fragen und rufen einander selbstständig zum Antworten auf (Fragekette).

1.7 Detecting irony and "So it goes."

Durch die Frage nach den ungewöhnlichen Eigenschaften des ersten Kapitels, von dem man gemeinhin erwartet, dass es als Exposition in die Handlung einführt , ergibt sich die Gelegenheit, Vonneguts komisch-ironischen Stil, seine Markenzeichen „dark irony and sarcasm" zu betrachten. Dabei werden die Schülerinnen und Schüler auch strukturelle Merkmale identifizieren, wie Wiederholungen und den berühmt gewordenen lakonischen Satz „So it goes". Diese Formel ist die stärkste Verweiskomponente im gesamten Werk.
Als Einstiegsimpuls wird nach ihrer Einschätzung über den Erzähler gefragt:

How do you feel about the narrator referring to himself as "an old fart" (cf. p. 2: "I have become an old fart with his memories and his Pall Malls…"; p. 7)?

Die Reaktion der Schülerinnen und Schüler kann Verlegenheit oder Entrüstung, aber auch ganz im Sinne des Autors Amüsement sein. Hier nimmt sich jemand selbst zurück, reduziert sich letztlich nur auf eine körperliche Ausscheidung, die noch nicht einmal mehr materiell ist, ein Gas, ein Wind – eine Nichtigkeit. Ernsthaft gedeutet arbeitet Vonnegut hier mit einem klassischen „pars pro toto" und krasser kann die Veranschaulichung dessen, was der Mensch angesichts des Todes ist, nicht sein. Das ist nicht nur komisch, das ist gehörige Selbstironie, auf die die Schülerinnen und Schüler wohl in ihren eigenen Worten selbst schnell kommen.

Eine kurze Begriffsklärung[1] zu „irony" und der bissig, scharfen Intensivierung des „sarcasm" kann der folgenden Aktivität vorausgeschickt und im Zusammenhang mit der Ankündigung der Gruppenarbeit an der Tafel gesichert werden:

Detecting irony and sarcasm in *Slaughterhouse-Five* (chapter 1)

irony = the amusing or strange aspect of a situation that is very different from what you expect; the use of words that say the opposite of what you really mean, often as a joke
sarcasm = a way of using words that is the opposite of what you mean in order to be unpleasant or even spiteful to sb or to ridicule them, or to expose inconvenient truths

Hieran knüpft eine längere textintensive arbeitsteilige Gruppenarbeit. Die Arbeitsanweisungen sollten vorher auf eine Folie übertragen werden. Dies erleichtert die Gruppenorganisation. Es sollen alle Passagen, in denen Ironie zu finden ist, aufgesucht, markiert und für eine Besprechung schriftlich zusammengefasst werden. Die Interpretation wird bei der Auswertung der Funde mündlich geleistet. Deutungsmöglichkeiten oder Kommentare für diese Ergebnissicherungsphase sind in der nachfolgenden Tabelle (S. 33 f.) in Klammern den Textstellenzitaten angefügt.

- Let's form four groups.
- Each group will deal with a text passage.
- Find funny, ironic, and sarcastic passages and write them down into your exercise books and on the transparency.
- Check the following pages.
  Group 1: pp. 1–5
  Group 2: pp. 6–9
  Group 3: pp. 10–13
  Group 4: pp. 14 to the end.

Es wäre ideal, wenn einigen Schülerinnen und Schüler die Bemerkung „So it goes" als ironischer Kommentar auffallen würde. Es kann aber sein, dass der Hinweis in die Lerngruppe gegeben werden muss.

Auswertungsphase und Ergebnissicherung

Die folgende Tabelle führt die Textstellen an und bietet in Klammern mögliche Kommentare bzw. Aspekte, die im Unterrichtsgespräch während und nach den individuellen Präsentationen als Deutungen herausgearbeitet werden können:

[1] irony, sarcasm, cf. Oxford Advanced Learners Dictionary

Text passages: comic reference, irony and sarcasm in Slaughterhouse-Five (ch.1)	
Group 1 p. 1	"All this happened, more or less." (Ironic message: either believe me or don't.)
p. 1	"A slaughterhouse was used as a prison for the captured soldiers." (Sarcasm: slaughtering animals during peacetime vs. manslaughter during war.)
p. 1	"G. Müller, the cab driver, had been a prisoner of the Americans." (Ironic coincidence.)
p. 2	"So it goes." (Ironic comment on a horrible death.)
p. 2	"I have become an old fart …" (Self-irony about his inability to write the Dresden novel.)
pp. 2–3	The limerick and the Yon Yonson song. (The irony lies in the fact that these stupid rhymes come to his mind when he ought to be thoroughly thinking and writing about the serious matter of the destruction of Dresden; yet, this is a significant expression of the endless repetition of war and, at the same time, history.)
p. 3	"Why don't you write an anti-glacier book instead?" (Irony: the filmmaker mocks the futility of anti-war books.)
pp. 3–4	"… that they were as easy to stop as glaciers. I believe that, too" (Self-irony: he agrees with Starr that he is a fool who thinks he can write a book against war, but obviously not against death.)
p. 4	"I have this disease late at night sometimes … I get drunk, and I drive my wife away with a breath like mustard gas and roses." (A comical self-confession that he reeks of a strange juxtaposition of smells – deathly war gas and the lovely smell of roses – when he is drunk.)
pp. 4–5	The irony of "poor old Edgar Derby" shall be "the climax of the book". O'Hare's reaction towards the narrator's enthusiasm is just "Um". (He talks about irony explicitly here; it is a comical situation because the narrator's expectations are dashed.)
p. 5	"As a trafficker in climaxes and thrills and characterizations …" (Self-irony: he mocks himself as a professional writer and teacher of creative writing who is not able to perform as easily as he should.)
p. 5	"The best outline I ever made … was on the back of a roll of wallpaper." (It is a comical idea imagining him sitting with that big roll of paper and using children's pens; it also shows irony as the story does not fit in the sense of the word used in its usual form and cannot be grasped in the usual way)
p. 5	"The end … was a beetfield on the Elbe … The rain … (Comic reference: at the end there is a plane field rather than anything highly dramatic.)
Group 2 p. 6	"So it goes." (Sarcasm: the laconic sentence reappears as a comment on Paul Lazzaro's looting of corpses in the burnt-out cellars of Dresden)
p. 7	"And we were flown to a rest camp … I married a pretty girl who was covered with baby fat, too" (Irony/sarcasm: first war wears out men and, afterwards, they are nourished like babies in the land of milk and honey, as if nothing had happened and as if the bad times had taken place in a different world. And from that seemingly untouched, healthy and sound world comes the fat girl who becomes his wife.)
p. 7	"And we had babies … I'm an old fart … I work in a lumbermill there". (Self-irony: the narrator recognizes that nothing special has become of him; he is just an average person)
p. 7	"And I let the dog out … and we talk some … He doesn't mind the smell of mustard gas and roses."(Comic reference/irony: Sandy, the dog is like a person, like a friend for him. She seems to be the only one to understand him – and there is the repetition of the smell!)

Text passages: comic reference, irony and sarcasm in Slaughterhouse-Five (ch.1)	
p. 8	"I was a student ... of Anthropology ... they were teaching that there was absolutely no difference between anybody. They may be teaching that still ... they taught ... that nobody was ridiculous or bad or disgusting ... I told him that was one of the things I learned in college after the war." (Irony/sarcasm: the science of humans and human behaviour is being ridiculed because the narrator has life experience proving that things are not as "splendid" as the books teach. The science of anthropology is outmoded.)
p. 8ff.	The story of the veteran who worked as an elevator-operator, got caught in the ornaments of the door by his wedding-ring formed of two lovebirds and was squashed to death. (The interpolated story is like a satire: the operator survived all the odds of war and then loses his life at his dreary job. The irony is that his wedding-ring is the reason for his fatal accident. The lovebirds are a symbol of never-ending love and staying together for a life-time. Death does not care about these kinds of lucky charms; it gets at people any time and any place. This incident is not only tragicomic in itself; the reaction of the narrator's boss Nancy is even more so. When he returns to the office, she is eating a candy bar undisturbed by the bloody message and even asks what the crushed man had looked like. This is more than pathetic of her. The narrator is astonished at this entire lack of sensibility. Comic reference: he points out that Nancy was eating a "Three Musketeers Candy Bar".)[1]
p. 9	"So it goes." appears for the third time to comment laconically on the cruel death of the operator (sarcasm).
Group 3 p. 11	"... that the information was top secret still... 'Secret? My God – from whom?'" (Irony: why should they keep the information secret from people who know it because they had been there in person? That is ridiculous or even macabre.)
p. 11	"We were United World Federalists back then. I don't know what we are now, Telephoners, I guess." (Self-irony/sarcasm: former social idealism has crumbled down to impersonal daily routines bereft of meaningful content.)
p. 13	"Mary had prepared an operating room." (Comic reference: since Mary did not like the narrator's visit, she did not make him feel comfortable. She let him know that he was not welcome and, instead of hospitability, she showed hostility towards him at the beginning.)
Group 4 p. 18	"We went to the New York World's Fair, saw what the past had been like, according to the Ford Motor Car Company and Walt Disney, saw what the future would be like, according to General Motors." (Sarcasm: a man's life-time is determined and defined by the mundane figures of the god Mammon, the economy and the media and not by spiritual powers anymore.)
p. 18	"I was not to be disturbed. I was working on my famous book about Dresden." (Self-irony and self-fulfilling prophesy: he mocks his own idea of becoming famous because he sees no progress in his writing and thinks it is too short, jumbled and jangled and a bad book. After all, he will have written a famous book about Dresden.)
p. 19	"... there is nothing intelligent to say about a massacre. Everybody is supposed to be dead, to never say anything or want anything ever again ... All there is to say about a massacre, things like 'Poo-tee-weet?'" (Gallows humour/black humour: the core message of Vonnegut's novel is that no sound human mind can understand the killing of fellow human beings.)
pp. 19– 20	"... I saw a lot of authentic backgrounds for made-up stories ... One of them will be 'Russian Baroque'... (Self-irony: he mocks himself and his silly ideas for new books, considering the titles to be lowbrow or banal, when he hasn't managed to finish his Dresden book, yet.)
p. 22	"I've finished my war book now. The next one I write is going to be fun. This one is a failure, and had to be, since it was written by a pillar of salt." (Self-irony: he refers to the bible story of Lot's wife whose fate he has cited before.)

Aus der sehr intensiven Texterarbeitungsphase und dem Kapitelende ergeben sich weitere Beobachtungsaufgaben für die Gesamtlektüre und die Dokumentation in den *Reading Companions*:

> What do you think about the ending of the first chapter?
>
> It is the beginning of the next chapter. Here we learn that Billy is "unstuck in time". This is a strange thing to be and very important for the novel. Otherwise it would not have been mentioned in such a prominent way. We also know from further reading that this is his problem or his fate.

Aufgrund dieser Beurteilung wird der Auftrag erteilt, alle "Zeitreisen" im Roman zu markieren und im *Reading Companion* gut zu dokumentieren.
Es soll eine erste Deutung der auffällig häufigen Wiederholung von „So it goes" versucht werden:

> What about the sentence "So it goes." and the fact that it is repeated?
>
> Student comments might include saying that it's short, it expresses resignation and frustration, it's laconic, a periodical repetition, iterated, etc.

Sie werden anschließend aufgefordert, beim Lesen auf weitere Vorkommen zu achten.[1] Sie sollen diese in ihren *Reading Companions* dokumentieren. Hierzu und zu weiteren sprachlichen oder stilistischen Besonderheiten erhalten sie ein Arbeitsblatt (***Copy 1, Symbolism and recurring motifs in Slaughterhouse-Five, S. 36***), auf dem sie ihre Beobachtungen für später dokumentieren können. Auf ***Copy 2*** (S. 37) sind die Lösungen bereits eingetragen.

Mit dem Arbeitsblatt wird gleichzeitig bewusst auf die wichtigsten Motive gelenkt, da von Schülerinnen und Schüler nicht erwartet wird, dass sie dies wie Studierende eigenständig leisten können. Da Vonnegut aber gerade wegen der ausgeklügelten Verweistechnik zu hohem literarischen Ansehen gelangte, ist die Aufmerksamkeit der Leserinnen und Leser unbedingt darauf zu schärfen.

[1] Der Satz erscheint 104mal. Die Schülerinnen und Schüler können sich den Spaß machen, genau zu zählen. Es wird auf alle Fälle klar, dass „So it goes" eine hochgradige Bedeutung in Bezug auf Aussage und Struktur des Werkes hat, die nach der Gesamtlektüre eine eigene Behandlung erfährt.

Symbolism and recurring motifs in *Slaughterhouse-Five*

- **Find the corresponding text passage and meaning for the depicted items.**

So it goes

The Children's Crusade:

[Bird] "Pooh-tee-weet":

"A smell like mustard gas and roses":

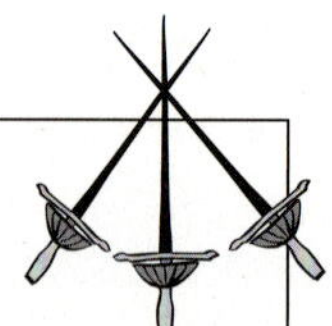

The Three Musketeers:

Colours

Orange and black:

Violet/purple:

Ivory and blue:

Dog:

To nestle like spoons:

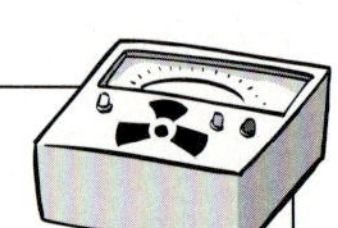

Radium dial:

Symbolism and recurring motifs in *Slaughterhouse-Five* (solutions)

- **Find the corresponding text passage and meaning for the depicted items.**

So it goes

pp. 2, 6, 7, 21, 22, 24, 25 (2x), 27, 32 (2x), 35, 36, 38, 41, 42, 45 (3x), 52, 53, 54, 62 (2x), 65, 68, 69, 73 (2x), 79 (2x), 81, 82 (2x), 83, 84, 89, 90 (2x), 91,92, 96, 99 (2x), 101 (2x), 103, 106 (2x), 109,112, 117, 128, 129, 135, 139, 140, 141,142, 143, 144, 145, 148, 149, 151 (2x), 156, 157 (2x), 159 (3x), 165, 167,171, 177 (2x), 178, 179,180, 183,187 (2x), 188, 196, 198 (2x), 200, 202, 203,204, 205 (4x), 210 (2x), 212 (4x), 214

The Children's Crusade:

pp. 106, 116 (schoolgirls); p. 131 (like a child); p. 148 (the hobo nestled like a spoon = fetal position); p. 149 (boys and men), pp. 157, 159 (the kitchen woman on the age of the soldiers) and p. 164 (Werner Gluck)

"Pooh-tee-weet":

pp. 19, 100, 215

"A smell like mustard gas and roses":

pp. 4, 7, 73

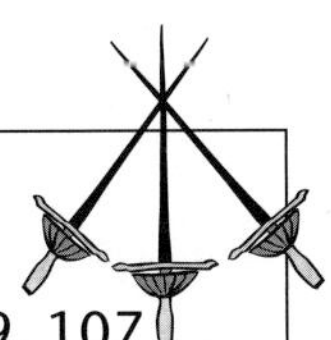

The Three Musketeers:

(Candy bar) pp. 9, 42, 43, 50, 54, 79, 107
(Candy bar) pp. 110, 156

Dog:

pp. 7, 48 (the German Dog);
p. 62 (spot the dog) p. 139 (Lazarro's perversity), p. 168 (a big dog barked); pp. 175, 177

To nestle like spoons:

pp. 70, 71 (Christmas in the boxcar);
p. 126 (Billy and Valencia);
p. 144 (Americans in the theatre performance of "Cinderella"); p. 148 (hobo); p. 160 (spooning was a crime)

Colours:

Orange and black:
p. 5 (orange: on the wall-paper for Dresden); p. 69 (boxcar); p. 72 (wedding-tent); p. 119

Violet/purple:
p. 43 (death); p. 76 (light of UFO)

Ivory and blue:
p. 65 (Billy's feet); pp. 72, 73, 74, 148 (hobo)

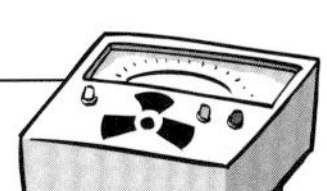

Radium dial:

pp. 82, 90, 91

Component 2

The historical background

Die Lektüre wird ab hier in häuslicher Vorbereitung fortgesetzt. Es wird mit der Lerngruppe ein realistischer Zeitraum für die Bewältigung eingedenk des Führens des *Reading Companions* und des Motiv-Beobachtungsbogens (s.o., *Copy 1*, S. 36) vereinbart. In dieser Zwischenzeit lässt sich die Aufbereitung des historischen Hintergrundes auf vielfältige Art und Weise gestalten.
Wenn im Vorfeld entsprechende Referate oder andere Präsentationen der Themen vereinbart wurden, wird man diese nun aktivieren.
Die folgende Unterrichtssequenz kann durch die Arbeit mit dem Internet entweder ganz gestaltet oder ergänzt werden. Im folgenden Verlauf wird an gegebener Stelle ein Hinweis auf den möglichen Einsatz der PCs gegeben. Er ist aber so konzipiert, dass auch ohne die Hilfe der Geräte das Hintergrundwissen sicher vermittelt wird. Die folgenden Informations- und Arbeitsblätter dienen hierzu, sie können natürlich auch als Stimulus oder Ergänzung für ein Computer-Projekt benutzt werden.

2.1 The war experience

Kurt Vonnegut hat als sehr junger Mann die Bombardierung Dresdens als deutscher Kriegsgefangener zum Ende des Zweiten Weltkrieges erlebt. Er schreibt seinen Roman in der Zeit, als wieder junge amerikanische Männer in einem Krieg traumatisiert werden und ihre Jugend, ihre Gesundheit, ihr Leben für den „Tanz mit dem Tod" geopfert haben. 1968 erreichte dieser mit der Tet-Offensive den Höhepunkt. Der verhängnisvolle Vietnam-Krieg gibt ihm Anlass, den Antikriegsroman endlich fertigzustellen. Besonders im letzten Kapitel werden diese zu seiner Zeit aktuellen politischen Zustände kritisiert.[1] Als *Slaughterhouse-Five* 1969 erschien, wurde es schnell von den amerikanischen Kriegsgegnern entdeckt und galt neben Hermann Hesses *Steppenwolf* als eine der „Bibeln" der Hippie- und *Flower Power* Bewegung.[2]
Zum Einfühlen in die Situation eines jugendlichen Soldaten und in die Figur des Billy Pilgrim und zur Hinführung zu diesem historischen Themenkomplex folgen einige kreative Vorschläge, die je nach Zeitrahmen alle oder in Auswahl durchgeführt werden können.
Hier eignet sich in besonderem Maße derHit „19" von Paul Hardcastle aus den 1980er-Jahren als motivierender, dynamischer Einstieg.
Es gibt diverse Vertonungen, die mit dem Text (***Copy 3, Paul Hardcastle: 19, S. 41***) besprochen werden können. Sehr empfehlenswert ist eine etwas zeitintensivere Beschäftigung mit dem Titel und seinen mannigfaltigen Versionen, wie sie z.B. auf *Youtube* zu sehen sind. Interessanterweise arbeitet Hardcastle genauso collagenhaft wie Vonnegut. Er setzt Interviewfetzen von Veteranen, Radionachrichten, Kriegsgeräusche zu einem Disco-hiphop-Beat und schafft so ein Kunstwerk, dem eigentlich größere Beachtung gebührt. Die vielen Adaptionen auf modernere Konflikte (Irak, Afghanistan), auch die deutsche Umsetzung, machen

[1] Eine Übersicht über die Rolle der USA im Zweiten Weltkrieg befindet sich im Anhang. Die Daten wurden in Bezug auf den Roman ausgewählt.

[2] Freese, Peter [Hrsg.]: *Der Roman im Englischunterricht der Sekundarstufe II: Theorie und Praxis*/Peter Freese ; Liesel Hermes (Hrsg.). – Paderborn: Schöningh, 1977, S. 311

betroffen. Die verzweifelte Aussage eines Offiziers „ I remember, when I look at my men, the average age was 19, my God you know, I'm taking boys to war"[1] aus dem Song unterstützt Vonneguts deterministische Erkenntnis "history keeps repeating itself". Seit Menschengedenken werden immer wieder Kinder in den Krieg geschickt, wie er mit dem extremsten historischen Beispiel, dem "Children's Crusade", gezeigt hat.[2]
Dem Einspielen geht die einfache Impulsfrage voraus:

How old are you? What do you think about the following song?

Im anschließenden Unterrichtsgespräch werden vielleicht einige Schülerinnen und Schüler erwähnen, dass ihre Großväter/Urgroßväter im Krieg gewesen sind. Oder man erfragt einfach, ob in der Familie jemand den zweiten Weltkrieg erlebt hat. Es kann nicht generell davon ausgegangen werden, dass alle die Möglichkeit haben, ein Interview mit einem Großelternteil diesbezüglich zu führen.
Je nachdem kann folgende Hausaufgabe gegeben werden. Die Schülerinnen und Schüler sollen ihre Verwandten nach ihren Kriegserlebnissen befragen. Dazu sollen sie möglichst viel Vokabular aus dem Wortfeld „ War and its aftermath" ***(Copy 4 Semantic field: war and its aftermath, S. 43)*** umsetzen. Das Vokabelblatt wird ihnen als Kopie ausgehändigt und sie erhalten die Anweisungen

1. Interview your grandparents or great grandparents on how they lived through the World War II years.
2. Use the vocabulary from the semantic field "war".

Alternativ kann diese Orientierungsaufgabe im eigenen Lebensumfeld auch als fiktiver Lebenslauf gestaltet werden. Dazu kann das Arbeitsblatt mit Bildern und Notizen eines deutschen Soldaten benutzt werden ***(Copy 5, From a German soldier's wartime photograph album, S. 44)***.
Die kreative Ausgestaltung kann auch als schriftliche Hausaufgabe gegeben werden.
Andere kreative Varianten zur Einstimmung auf die Kriegsumstände könnten die Wiedergabe von Eindrücken aus einem Kriegsfilm[3] sein oder das Erstellen einer Fotowand.
Dazu sollen die Schülerinnen und Schüler ein oder zwei Bilder aus Zeitschriften oder dem Internet (Quellennachweise einfordern!) mitbringen, die entweder als Wandzeitung beschriftet werden, oder von allen zu einer Collage zusammengefügt werden, die anschließend mündlich und schriftlich beschrieben werden kann. Letztere Aktion kann thematisch eng am Zweiten Weltkrieg oder weiter generell an Kriegen in der Welt ausgerichtet werden.

2.2 Dresden and the Battle of the Bulge

Mit dem Arbeitsblatt auf ***Copy 6 "The war locations"***, S. 45 erhalten die Schülerinnen und Schüler eine Vorstellung von den Gebieten, um die es sich im Roman hauptsächlich handelt. Die erste Aufgabe kann direkt aus dem Kartenmaterial gelöst werden. Die beiden anderen gehen darüber hinaus. Zur Lösungsfindung kann direkt mit dem Informationsblatt ***(Copy 7, The Battle of the Bulge and The Bombing of Dresden, S. 46)*** gearbeitet werden.

---

1 Paul Hardcastle, Boys to War, the 25th anniversary edition (8.2.2013)

2 Die Schülerinnen und Schüler mögen auch auf Kindersoldaten, wie sie auch z. B. durch den Bürgerkrieg in Uganda um den Milizführer Joseph Kony in seiner „ Widerstandsarmee des Herrn" in den Medien gezeigt wurden, kommen. Das brisante Thema muss hier wohl auf die *Post-reading*-Phase verschoben werden, wenn man den eigentlichen thematischen Rahmen nicht überdehnen will.

3 Anregungen siehe „Weiterführende Literatur und Medien", S. 127

Es bietet sich allerdings an, mit der Klasse eine Internet-Recherche vorzunehmen oder in arbeitsteiliger Form einzelne Schülerinnen und Schüler oder Gruppen innerhalb einer solchen Projektarbeit mit der Lösung zu beauftragen. Eine andere Variante, besonders, wenn die Möglichkeit zur gemeinsamen Recherche an Computern nicht gegeben ist, wäre es, genauso arbeitsteilig zu verfahren und die Aufgabe häuslich erledigen zu lassen. Zur nächsten Stunde sind dann von den „Experten" die entsprechenden Antworten zu liefern.
Schülerinnen und Schüler, die sich im Umgang mit Internet-Recherchen auskennen, werden den einfachsten Weg zur Informationsbeschaffung gehen: In eine Suchmaschine werden die Begriffe „Dresden" und „Battle of the Bulge" eingegeben. Entscheiden Sie vorher, ob die Schülerinnen und Schüler auch deutschsprachiges Material benutzen sollen oder dürfen. Da sie die Lösungen sowieso auf Englisch formulieren müssen, ist dies durchaus zulässig. Das Problem hierbei liegt auf der Metaebene, oft kippen solche Stunden dann zu vorwiegend auf Deutsch geführten Gesprächen.

Empfehlenswerte Internetseiten sind neben „Wikipedia": www.britannica.com; www.einestages.spiegel.de; http://www.history.com/topics/battle-of-the-bulge; diverse Einstellungen aus Dokumentarfilmen finden sich auch auf *Youtube*.

Die Aufbereitung in Wikipedia mit Bildern, Zeitzeugendokumenten, etc. ist ein hervorragendes Studienobjekt und ihre Auswertung kann schon für die Aufgabe genügen, wohl unter dem Hinweis an die Schülerinnen und Schüler, dass das *Online-Lexikon* nicht generell als alleinige Informationsquelle benutzt werden sollte und Artikel ohne kritischen Apparat hinterfragt werden müssten.

Paul Hardcastle: 19 (1985)

(War protestants)
(Peter Thomas) In 1965 Vietnam seemed like just another foreign war,
but it wasn't.
It was different in many ways, as so were those that did the fighting.
In World War II the average age of the combat soldier was 26…
In Vietnam he was 19.
In ininininininin Vietnam he was 19.
(TV announcer's voice)
The shooting and fighting of the past two weeks continued today
25 miles west of Saigon
(Veteran)
I really wasn't sure what was going on
(Veteran)
Nininini Nineteen, 19, Ni-nineteen 19
19,19,19,19
In Vietnam the combat soldier typically served a twelve month tour of duty but
was exposed to hostile fire almost every day
Nininininininininininin 19 nininininninin 19
(Reporter)
Hundreds of Thousands of men who saw heavy combat in Vietnam were arrested
since discharge
Their arrest rate is almost twice that of non-veterans of the same age.
There are no accurate figures of how many of these men have been incarcerated.
But, a Veterans Administration study concludes that the greater of Vets
exposure to combat could more likely affect his chances of being arrested or
convicted.
This is one legacy of the Vietnam War
(Singing Girls)
All those who remember the war
They won't forget what they've seen…
Destruction of men in their prime
whose average age was 19
Dededededededede-Destruction
Dededededededede-Destruction
War, War ….
(Reporter)
After World War II the men came home together on troop ships, but the Vietnam
Vet often arrived home within 48 hours of jungle combat
Perhaps the most dramatic difference
between World War II and Vietnam was
coming home.. .none of them received a hero's welcome/None of them received a
hero's welcome
None of them received a hero's welcome, none of them, none of them
Nenene Nenene None of them, none of them, none of them …
None of them received a hero's welcome
(Reporter)
According to a Veteran's Administration study
Half of the Vietnam combat veterans suffered from what psychiatrists call
Post-Traumatic-Stress-Disorder
Many vets complain of alienation, rage, or guilt
Some succumb[6] to suicidal thoughts
Eight to Ten years after coming home almost eight-hundred-thousand men are

discharge *Entlassung*
incarcerated imprisoned
legacy *Vermächtnis*
prime *Blüte(zeit)*
alienation *Entfremdung*
succumb surrender to

still fighting the Vietnam War
(Singing Girls)
Dedededededede-Destruction
Nininininininininin Nineteen, 19, Ni-nineteen 19
19,19,19,19
Nininininininininin Nineteen, 19, Ni-nineteen 19
19,19,19,19
(Soldier)
When we came back it was different.. Everybody wants to know „How'd it
happened to those guys over there
There's gotta be something wrong somewhere
We did what we had to do
There's gotta be something wrong somewhere
People wanted us to be ashamed of what it made us
Dad had no idea what he went to fight and he is now
All we want to do is come home
All we want to do is come home
What did we do it for
All we want to do is come home
Was it worth it?

Semantic field: war and its aftermath

to declare war on sb *jmd. den Krieg erklären*	a conventional/nuclear war	enemy *Feind*, enmity, hostility *Feindschaft*, hostile *feindlich*	wartime comrade, war buddy
to wage war on sb *Krieg gegen jmd führen*, to wage a war on two fronts	to spread war over a country	ambush, to be ambushed	soldier returning from the war *Kriegsheimkehrer(in)*
to be at war with sb/a country	to be killed in action/in the war *im Krieg gefallen sein*	court martial *Kriegsgericht/ Standgericht*, to court-martial sb. *jmden vor ein Krigesgericht stellen*	post-traumatic war syndrom, traumatized by war *kriegstraumatisiert*
To be constantly feuding with sb/to be constantly at loggerheads with sb *in einem ständigen Krieg stehen mit*	to go to war, to enter war	warfare, conduct of war *Kriegsführung*, psychological warfare	(war) veteran, war (veteran) memorial *Kriegerdenkmal*
warring, belligerent *Krieg führend*, a belligerent country	battle, combat, war operation	warrior, combatant	war disabled person, disabled ex-serviceman *Kriegsversehrte/r*
bomb strike/attack *Bombenangriff*	to arm for war *aufrüsten*, arming, amament, nuclear armament, the acquisition of nuclear/ conventional arms	war refugee, refugee camp, refuge *Zuflucht*, displaced persons, deportee, expellees from his/ her homeland *Vertriebene*	war widow, war orphan *Kriegswaise*, war victim's pension *Kriegsopferrente*
bomb release, bombing *Bombenabwurf*, to blanket-bomb *etw mit einem dichten Bombenteppich belegen*, hail of bombs *Bombenhagel*	outbreak of war start of war readiness for war	POW prisoner of war, to become a prisoner of war *in Kriegsgefangenschaft geraten*	bereaved family, the/sb's surviving dependants *Hinterbliebene* surving dependant's pension *Hinterbliebenenrente*, provision for dependants *Hinterbliebenenversorgung*
shrapnel, bomb splinter *Bombensplitter*	war cries *Kriegsgeschrei*, warmongering *Kriegshetze*, *Stimmungsmache für einen Krieg*, warmonger *Kriegstreiber*	captivity *Kriegsgefangenschaft*, detention camp *Internierungslager*	pacifist *Kriegsgegner*
curfew *Ausgangssperre*, to impose a curfew	Battlefield, battleground, war zone, war arena, theatre of war/ operations *Kriegsschauplatz*	war-weary *kriegsmüde*, combat fatigue *Kriegsmüdigkeit*, to desert the army, to desert to the enemy *zum Feind überlaufen*	a conscientious objector *Kriegsdienstverweigerer*, conscientious objection *Kriegsdienstverweigerung*
air raid bunker *Luftschutzbunker*, cellar used as an air raid shelter *Luftschutzkeller*	war atrocities *Kriegsgräuel*, war crime, war criminal, war crimes tribunal to suffer heavy losses *schwere Verluste erleiden* war victims *Kriegsopfer* war wound *Kriegsverletzung*, violation of human rights *Menschenrechtsverletzung*	to do one's military duty *den/ seinen Wehrdienst leisten*, person doing his/her mandatory military service *Wehrdienstleistende/r*, fit for military service *wehrdiensttauglich*, to be drafted for military service *zum Wehrdienst einberufen werden*	to compensate, to make up for sth *wiedergutmachen*, compensation *Wiedergutmachung*, restoration of buildings, re-establishment of a government *Wiederherstellung*, improvement costs *Wiederherstellungskosten*, reparation payments *Reparationszahlungen*
strategem *Kriegslist*, (high) treason *(Hoch)verrat*, retaliatory strike *Vergeltungsangriff*	to impose martial law *das Kriegsrecht verhängen*	to hold a (high) rank, to be a high-ranking officer *einen (hohen) militärischen Rang bekleiden*	victory, victorious power *Siegermacht*
armistice *Waffenstillstand*, ceasefire *Waffenruhe, Feuerpause*	navy *Kriegsmarine*, fleet, infantry *Fußtruppe*, artillery *schwere Geschütztruppe*, tank or armoured division *Panzerdivision*, anti-tank defence *Panzerabwehr*, bazooka *Panzerfaust*, air force *Luftwaffe*	to disarm *entwaffnen, abrüsten*, disarmament *Abrüstung*, disarmament talks/negotiations	peace negotiations, to sign a peace treaty *einen Friedensvertrag unterzeichnen*, human rights *Menschenrechte*, human dignity *Menschenwürde*
war-hungry *kriegslüstern*	warring party/faction *Kriegspartei*	war correspondent *Kriegsberichterstatter*	War Graves Commission *Kriegsgräberfürsorge*

From a German soldier's wartime photograph album

On this photograph, the German soldier is 18 years old and serves as a foreman in France in 1943. He belongs to the crew of a Ju-52 aircraft and works as a radio operator. At the end of the war there are no more machines, and he has to walk home in the retreat from Russia.

- **Write his story using the photographs below in your composition.**

What might he have seen? What might he have felt? What might he think about war today?

1. Military training

2. The crew on the job

3. Killed in action – the comrades of the "sister machine"

4. Frozen face in Russia – no planes and no equipment anymore

5. A long walk home – retreating from Russia on foot

The war locations

In the novel *Slaughterhouse-Five,* Billy Pilgrim fights in the Battle of the Bulge in Luxembourg. He gets lost behind German lines and is captured. As a prisoner of war (POW), he is first imprisoned at a prison camp in the Chemnitz area and is then deported to Dresden in the boxcar of a train.

The Battle of the Bulge – Luxembourg 1944/45

Germany in World War II

1. Describe the movement of the US front line from 15 December 1944 to 7 February 1945.
2. Find out more about the last major German offensive in the Ardennes.
3. Get information on Dresden before the war and the destruction. What is the historical explanation for the air raid, and how many victims were there really?
4. What is Dresden like nowadays?

The Battle of the Bulge and the bombing of Dresden (information)

The Battle of the Bulge (December 16, 1944–Janaury 28, 1945)

In December 1944, in an all-out gamble to compel the Allies to sue for peace, Adolf Hitler ordered the only major German counteroffensive of the war in northwest Europe. Its objective was to split the Allied armies by means of a surprise blitzkrieg thrust through the Ardennes to Antwerp [...] Despite Germany's historical penchant for mounting counteroffensives when things looked darkest, the Allies' leadership miscalculated and left the Ardennes lightly defended by only two inexperienced and two battered American divisions.

On December 16, three German armies (more than a quarter-million troops) launched the deadliest and most desperate battle of the war in the west in the poorly roaded, rugged, heavily forested Ardennes. The once-quiet region became bedlam as American units were caught flat-footed and fought desperate battles to stem the German advance at St.-Vith, Elsenborn Ridge, Houffalize and, later, Bastogne, which was defended by the 101st Airborne Division. The inexperienced U.S. 106th Division was nearly annihilated, but even in defeat helped buy time for Brigadier General Bruce C. Clarke's brilliant defense of St.-Vith. As the German armies drove deeper into the Ardennes in an attempt to secure vital bridgeheads west of the River Meuse quickly, the line defining the Allied front took on the appearance of a large protrusion or bulge, the name by which the battle would forever be known.

A crucial German shortage of fuel and the gallantry of American troops fighting in the frozen forests of the Ardennes proved fatal to Hitler's ambition to snatch, if not victory, at least a draw with the Allies in the west. Lieutenant General George S. Patton's remarkable feat of turning the Third Army ninety degrees from Lorraine to relieve the besieged town of Bastogne was the key to thwarting the German counteroffensive. The Battle of the Bulge was the costliest action ever fought by the U.S. Army, which suffered over 100,000 casualties.

to sue for peace to ask for peace

to have a penchant for sth *Einen Hang zu etw/ eine Vorliebe für etw haben*

rugged uneven and bumpy
bedlam chaos

106th Division = Vonnegut's division

protrusion *Vorsprung*
bulge *Vorsprung, Beule, hier: Anhöhe*
crucial important

feat brave deed

to thwart to prevent sb from doing sth

Shortened from : CARLO W. D'ESTE The Reader's Companion to Military History. Edited by Robert Cowley and Geoffrey Parker.

URL: http://www.history.com/topics/battle-of-the-bulge (Aufruf: 10.2.2013)

The Bombing of Dresden

was an attack on the city of Dresden, the capital of the German state of Saxony, that took place in the final months of the Second World War. In four raids between 13 and 15 February 1945, 722 heavy bombers of the British Royal Air Force (RAF) and 527 of the United States Army Air Forces (USAAF) dropped more than 3,900 tons of high-explosive bombs and incendiary devices on the city. The resulting firestorm destroyed fifteen square miles (39 square kilometres) of the city centre. At least 22,000, at most 25,000 people were killed. Post-war discussion of whether or not the attacks were justified has led to the bombing becoming one of the moral *causes célèbres* of the Second World War.

incendiary causing fire

cause célèbre an issue that attracts a lot of attention

Excerpt from Wikipedia (23.1.2013)

Component 3

The autobiographical background – who is Billy Pilgrim?

Es wird erwartet, dass die Schülerinnen und Schüler das Buch nun ganz gelesen haben und mit ihren *Reading Companions* fähig sind, den Text thematisch zu bearbeiten.

3.1 Who is Kurt Vonnegut?

Der Erzähler fordert am Ende des Kapitels recht autoritativ auf, zuzuhören. Er zitiert den Anfang seiner Geschichte und so erfährt der Leser, dass die Geschichte einen Helden namens Billy Pilgrim haben wird. Das ist unerwartet, da der Erzähler im ersten Kapitel ausführlich davon sprach, dass er seine eigenen Dresden-Erlebnisse niederschreiben wollte. Wer ist der Erzähler eigentlich und wer ist Billy Pilgrim?
Die Schülerinnen und Schüler können den schillernd-skurrilen Schriftsteller, Kurt Vonnegut, am besten kennenlernen, indem sie ihn sehen und hören. Möglich wird dies durch etliche Filmdokumentationen, die z. B. auf *Youtube* zu sehen sind, wenn man nur „Kurt Vonnegut" eingibt.[1] Wenn hierzu keine Möglichkeit besteht, kann die Live-Aufnahme auf der Hör-CD einen Klangeindruck verschaffen.
Die optische Präsentation der sehr individuellen Erscheinung des wuschelköpfigen Autors kann mit der Abbildung erfolgen, die Vonnegut mit der Tapetenrolle zeigt, die er im ersten Kapitel als Mittel zur Strukturierung des Romans erwähnt zeigt. Dazu kann das Foto von ***Copy 10, Travelling in time – instructions for analysing the structure, S. 62*** auf Folie vergrößert werden.
Nach der Besprechung der Eindrücke zum Autor erhalten die Schülerinnen und Schüler ein Arbeitsblatt zur Biografie Kurt Vonneguts (***Copy 8, Who is Kurt Vonnegut?, S. 52)*** und sollen, nachdem der Text laut gelesen wurde, die Aufgabe

Compare Vonnegut's life to the narrator's life and Billy Pilgrim in the novel.

in zwei Etappen erfüllen:

1. Die Parallelen werden in Partnerarbeit unterstrichen. Eine Farbe kennzeichnet dabei Ähnlichkeiten mit dem, was der Erzähler sagte. Dazu ziehen die Schülerinnen und Schüler ihre früher angefertigte Sammlung heran (siehe S. 27 f.). Eine andere Farbe kennzeichnet, was sie aufgrund ihrer Lektüre und dem Nachschlagen in ihren *Reading Companions* über Billy Pilgrims Leben wissen.

Die Tabelle gibt die Textstellen wieder und erklärt über das für die Schülerinnen und Schüler Offensichtliche weitere Bezüge, die von der Lehrkraft ergänzt werden können:

[1] z.B. Kurt Vonnegut, on how to write a short story (*Youtube*-Zugriff: 12.2.13). Hier liest er sein „Rezept", das sehr aufschlussreich auch in Bezug auf die Struktur von *Slaughterhouse-Five* ist, zu Bildern aus seinem Leben. Aus den vielen anderen Kurzfilmen muss man selbst eine Auswahl treffen oder den Schülerinnen und Schülern den Tipp geben, selbst einmal darin zu „schmökern".

Text: Who is Kurt Vonnegut?	Author-narrator (Ch.1)	Billy Pilgrim; other traces
ll. 10ff.: Vonnegut's father was an architect.		Billy's father was a barber. (p. 110)
ll. 19ff.: But before he became engaged in war and its atrocities, he made his way through high school. After brief training as a mechanical engineer, the army sent him back to college. When men were needed, he was sent to the infantry, doing service as a battalion intelligence scout on the German-Luxembourgian border.		Billy Pilgrim does the same, finishes like Vonnegut, after coming home. Billy is there, too. The difference is that Vonnegut has changed his function to the non-violent service of an assistant to a chaplain.[1]
ll. 32ff.: In 1944, he was taken prisoner during the Battle of the Bulge serving in the unfortunate 106th Division. He survived the bombardment of Dresden, where he had been kept imprisoned, with a group of other American POWs in a former meat locker. Vonnegut worked at a liquid vitamin factory and he had to gather up and burn the remains of the dead after the inferno.	This is the author-narrator's main subject, the reason for writing the book.	Billy's war experience is exactly the same: • imprisonment during the Battle of the Bulge • survival in the meat locker • working at the syrup factory • disposing the corpses after the bombing, as hard labour
ll. 38ff.: After his return to the USA, he first tried to re-establish himself as a student of anthropology at the University of Chicago. He earned his living by working as a reporter for the Chicago News Bureau at the same time.	This is stated by the author-narrator as well.	The study of anthropology has certainly influenced his idea of the Tralfamadorians, their attitude towards time and life, and their philosophy and interest in Charles Darwin's evolution.
ll. 47ff.: The first novel was a failure; he sold short stories to some science fiction magazines and sold cars.	He has problems in writing the book.	The science fiction novelist Kilgore Trout appears to be transferred from Kurt Vonnegut: as he is not successful, he has to sell newspapers to make a living.
ll. 51ff.: In 1957, he lost three beloved members of the family: first his father died. ll. 53ff.: Then his brother-in-law was killed in a train accident only two days before his wife, Vonnegut's sister, died of cancer at the age of 40.		These blows of fate are the foil for what happens to Billy: however, his father dies more "dignified" in a hunting accident. The incredible coincidence of these two unexpected deaths in such a short time were the foil for Billy's plane crash and Valencia's fatal mad driving to the hospital.

[1] Aus dem Interview auf der CD ist zu erfahren, dass Vonnegut ein Vorbild für die Gestalt des Billy Pilgrim hatte. Es war sein Kamerad Edgar Coone. Das kann jetzt, aber auch noch später erwähnt werden.

[ll. 54 ff.: Vonnegut adopted his sister's children and was now father of six]	The author-narrator has a daughter.	Billy is shown as a loving family man. He finds salvation and happiness with his family. When Valencia dies, he creates a "new family" for himself, first with the Tralfamadorians, who care for him as if he were their own child. Then he starts creating a new family in "Adam and Eve" style with Montana. The idea of this utopian restart of the human species is said to be due to Vonnegut's anthropological studies and his distinctive sense of family.[1]
ll. 59 ff.: A Guggenheim Fellowship award made it possible for him to return to Dresden to prepare *Slaughterhouse-Five.*	The author-narrator appreciates this award a great deal.	Billy Pilgrim does not return to Dresden after the war.
	The author-narrator warns his sons never ever to get involved in massacre.	Billy Pilgrim is different. He is proud of his son Robert being a Green Beret soldier and fighting as a patriot in Vietnam. Billy Pilgrim does not protest against that war and seems still to be a patriotic soul.

2. Anschließend formulieren die Schülerinnen und Schüler in Einzelarbeit, gegebenenfalls zu Hause, den Vergleich als zusammenhängenden Text.
Aus den Vergleichen zeigt sich, dass Vonnegut sowohl den Erzähler als auch Billy Pilgrim als fiktive Figuren mit einigen wahren, aber auch erfundenen Eigenschaften versehen hat.[2] Der Erzähler erzeugt mit seiner ständigen Präsenz einen Rahmen, der Billys Geschichte realistisch erscheinen lässt. Mehrmals taucht Vonnegut in direkten Erzählerkommentaren wie eine Stimme aus dem „Off" im Roman auf[3] und einmal ruft er Billy Pilgrim sogar an (cf. p. 73). Billy trägt viele autobiografische Züge, wird aber durch die Eigenschaft des „Zeitreisens" zu einer Gestalt für Vonneguts ethische und politische Mitteilungsabsichten. Wer ist also Billy Pilgrim?

3.2 Characterizing Billy Pilgrim

Das zweite Kapitel bietet einen detaillierten Bericht über Billy Pilgrims Leben. Es bietet sich an, eine erste „Grobansicht" der Person herauszuarbeiten. Die hierfür relevanten Textstellen (p. 23–25) sollen beim gemeinsamen abschnittsweisen lauten Lesen oder dem Mitlesen zur

[1] Merrill Robert and Peter A. Scholl, Vonnegut's Slaughterhouse-Five: The Requirements of Chaos, in Studies in American Fiction, Vol. 6, No. 1, Spring, 1978

[2] Vonnegut hatte zudem seinen Kameraden, Edgar Crone, als Vorbild für Billy. Dies ist in dem Interview auf der CD zu erfahren. Viele authentische Einzelheiten, wie diese, können in Veteranenberichten wie z.B. „Local vet recalls his POW days with the late Kurt Vonnegut 2007-05-03 By Daniel Sturm Athens NEWS Contributor „auf der Homeage der „Indiana Military Organization" http://www.indianamilitary.org/ – German POW Camps – Slaughterhouse-Five – Vonnegut, Karl [sic!] (25.5.2013) nachgelesen werden.

[3] Vgl. Copy 11, Travelling in time … (solution), S. 63 ff.

CD (CD 1/ T4), markiert und ggf. nach Klärung von Verständnisfragen an der Tafel gesammelt werden. Die Ausformulierung kann in Einzelarbeit oder Partnerarbeit anschließend oder als Hausaufgabe geschehen.

Who is Billy Pilgrim? Characterize him referring to chapter 2, pp. 23–25.

Mögliche Ergebnisse an der Tafel, aus denen die Charakterisierung formuliert werden soll:

Billy Pilgrim (ch. 2)

- He has come unstuck in time. (p. 23) p. 27
- He is a senile widower.
- He is "spastic" to time.
- In a constant state of fright, because he never knows in what part of his life he will be next.
- He had been a funny-looking child and youth: tall and weak, and shaped like a bottle of Coca-Cola.
- He had been very good at high school.
- He had attended night sessions at the Ilium School of Optometry before being drafted for military service in WWII (p. 24).
- He suffered a mild nervous collapse after his honourable discharge from the army and his engagement.
- He was shock treated at a veteran's hospital.
- He recovered and was able to marry, finish his education, and be set up in business by his father-in-law.
- He was good at his job and became rich.
- He became the father of Barbara and Robert.
- He claimed to have been kidnapped by Tralfamadorians after a plane crash accident (p. 25).

Neben der Fertigstellung der Charakterisierung soll Kapitel 2 bis zur nächsten Stunde noch einmal auf die Lebensdaten hin gescannt werden. Dazu kann der *Reading Companion* gute Dienste leisten, wenn er gepflegt wurde.

Anhand der Datenfülle im zweiten Kapitel lässt sich Billys Leben von seiner Geburt 1922 an bis hin zu seiner „Entführung" durch die Tralfamadorianer recht gut chronologisch verfolgen. Eine lineare Darstellung hilft zudem der Orientierung, die durch die erwähnten und im Folgenden ausgeführten Zeitsprünge auch guten Schülern verloren gehen kann.
Dazu kann zeitöknomisch vorgegangen werden, wenn man den oberen Teil der Zeitstrahltabelle auf die Tafel oder eine Folie zur Beschriftung überträgt (***Copy 9, Billy Pilgrim's life in chronological order, S. 54)*** oder die Tabelle kopiert, die Lösungen herauslöscht und nur das Gerüst zum Ausfüllen als Kopie verteilt.

Find out about Billy's real life and draw a chronological timeline.

Billy Pilgrim's Life

1922–1944	1944–1945	1945–1948	1957–1966	1967	1968

Das Eintragen der Daten geschieht dann gemeinsam im entsprechenden fragend-entwickelnden Unterrichtsgespräch. (Lösung siehe ***Copy 9, Billy Pilgrim's Life, S. 54)***

Billy begegnet uns, obwohl erst 46 Jahre alt, als „senile widower" 1968. Das ist seine Gegenwart. Er behauptet immer wieder von sich selbst, er sei losgelöst von der Zeit („unstuck in time"). Der Erzähler erklärt seinen Zustand als Spastik, als unkontrollierte und durchaus nicht angenehme Eigenschaft. Er erlebt sein Leben immer und immer wieder von der Geburt bis zum Tod. Die Schülerinnen und Schüler sollen die Vorstellung, die sich aus dem ersten Absatz des zweiten Kapitels ergibt, als Skizze darstellen. Es könnte ein spiralförmiges Gebilde entstehen, auf dem oder in dem sich Billy allerdings wie durch einen Zufallsgenerator mal hier, mal dort befindet. Das kann durch eine Sprungbewegung gezeigt werden (mit der Kreide oder dem Stift auf der Spirale o. Ä.). Wenn die Örtlichkeit es erlaubt, könnte eine solche Spirale auch auf dem Boden gezeichnet und durch eine/n springenden Schüler/in dargestellt werden.

Who is Kurt Vonnegut?

Norman Mailer, one of the most popular American writers, is said to have hailed Vonnegut as "a marvelous writer with a style that remained undeniably and imperturbably his own" and that he would "salute him as our own Mark Twain". Such praise had not always been bestowed on Vonnegut.

to hail *here:* to praise

imperturbable *here: unverwechselbar*

His ideas and attitudes are rooted in his upbringing in Indianapolis, Indiana, where he was born into a wealthy and cultured family of architects stemming from the third generation of German immigrants. His parents did not teach him German because they were afraid of the widespread anti-German sentiment at that time. He was raised in a liberal atmosphere of scepticism and humanistic atheism. It must have been fate that he was born on 11 November 1922, which is Armistice Day – a meaningful coincidence. But before he became engaged in war and its atrocities, he made his way through high school.

Armistice Day *Volkstrauertag* (**armistice** *Waffenstillstand*)
atrocity cruel and violent act

The 1940s turned out to be the crucial period in setting the scene for his future life and career. Following his father's advice, he studied chemistry and biology at the Cornell University in Ithaca, New York. There, he joined the student newspaper and developed his particular brand of humour, also spreading his pacifist ideas.

crucial important

But that came to an abrupt end when Pearl Harbor was bombed in 1941. Vonnegut's life changed dramatically. He enlisted in the US Army as a volunteer and was trained to operate a 240-millimeter howitzer. After a brief training as a mechanical engineer, the army sent him back to college until men were needed. Later, he was sent to the infantry, doing service as a battalion intelligence scout at the German-Luxembourgian border.

howitzer *Haubitze*

intelligence scout *Späher*

Vonnegut was not home when his mother committed suicide in 1944. At that time, he was taken prisoner in the Battle of the Bulge, serving in the unfortunate 106th Division. He survived the bombardment of Dresden where he had been kept imprisoned, with a group of other American POWs, in a former meat locker. Vonnegut worked at a liquid vitamin factory, and he had to gather up and burn the remains of the dead after the inferno.

After his return to the USA, he first tried to re-establish himself as a student of anthropology at the University of Chicago. He earned his living by working as a reporter for the Chicago News Bureau at the same time. Unfortunately, he did not obtain his degree because his Master's thesis ('Fluctuations Between Good and Evil in Simple Tales') was rejected. He left the academic world and took a job in public relations for General Electric. Finding it hard to cope with what he called "the capitalist hypocrisy of the American business", he quit the job in 1951 and moved with the family he had by then to Cape Cod, Massachusetts to become a full-time writer.

hypocrisy *Heuchelei*

The 1950s are a period of personal grief and trauma.

His first novel *Player Piano* (1952) was a failure. He sold short stories to some science fiction magazines but had to additionally take on several jobs like teaching English at a school for emotionally disturbed children, working as an advertising agent, and selling cars.

In 1957, he lost three beloved members of his family: first his father died. He had fallen

into deep depression and, after becoming completely mentally unstable, had lived in a sanatorium.
Then his brother-in-law was killed in a train accident only two days before his wife, Vonnegut's sister, died of cancer at the age of 40. The couple left three children. Vonnegut adopted them and was now father of six, which put enormous financial strain on him and his wife. He was still not recognized as a serious writer.
In the late 1960s, his popularity began to grow on college campuses and among the liberal communities of New York and San Francisco, gaining him the badge of a "cult" author. A Guggenheim Fellowship award made it possible for him to return to Dresden to prepare *Slaughterhouse-Five*.
Vonnegut died in 2007 after a fall in his house. Some newspapers commented on this unexpected death in the only appropriate manner, citing his famous line from *Slaughterhouse-Five*: "So it goes."

badge mark

to cite to quote

1. Compare Vonnegut's life to the narrator's life and Billy Pilgrim in the novel.
2. Where else do you find traces of autobiography in the novel?

Solution sheet

Billy Pilgrim's life (in chronological order, cf. Chapter 2)

1922–1944	1944–1945	1945–1948	1957–1966	1967	1968
1922: Birth in Ilium, New York He visits the Grand Canyon and Carlsberg Caverns with his parents. He attends high school and night classes at the Ilium School of Optometry.	December of 1944: Battle of the Bulge in Luxembourg 1944: Billy experiences his first "time jump", and from then on he is in a permanent loop of time travel. He is a POW in Germany at Chemnitz and Dresden; he witnesses the bombing on 14 February 1945 while imprisoned in Slaughterhouse Five. He returns to the USA thanks to a prisoners' exchange.	1945: after his discharge from the Army, he completes studies at the Ilium School of Optometry He becomes engaged to Valencia Merble. Veteran's hospital at Lake Placid Shock treatment Marriage	In 1957, he is a member of the Lion's club. In 1965, his mother is in an old people's home. In 1966, it is his18th wedding anniversary.	He is kidnapped by a flying saucer on Barbara's wedding day.	Air plane crash
Childhood and youth	War	He is a prospering optometrist and father of two children. = A phase of being settled as a bourgeois civilian.		1966: he begins to display strange behaviour and signs of probable dementia in public.	

Component 4

"There is no way to express massacre" – time travel and structure

Den Auftakt zum Projekt der Strukturanalyse kann ein kreativer Einstieg („scattered dialogues") machen. Es soll in freier Assoziation ein spontanes kleines Bühnenstück entstehen.
Vorbereitung:

- Im Zimmer wird ein Raum als „Bühne" frei geräumt.
- Die Schülerinnen und Schüler erhalten zehn Minuten Zeit, einen vierzeiligen Dialog auf Zettel zu schreiben.
- Diese Zettel werden dann auf dem Boden der Bühne durcheinandergeworfen.
- Gruppen zu je drei Schülerinnen und Schüler werden gebildet.
- Der Auftrag lautet:

> - Perform an improvised scene. Whenever you get stuck, pick up a piece from the papers that are scattered around you and recite the dialogue and try to integrate it in your play as well as possible.

Nach zwei oder drei Aufführungen werden die Schülerinnen und Schüler nach ihrem Erleben befragt. Es geht weniger um den sinnvollen Inhalt als um das Nachempfinden der Vonnegut'schen Methode der freien Assoziation bzw. des *stream-of-consciousness*-Erlebnisses. Die Gefühle werden gemischt sein, man hat sich vielleicht albern gefühlt, dann doch beflügelt, etwas aus den Fetzen machen zu wollen, war dann erstaunt, dass es irgendwie einen Sinn ergab und dass dabei das Verknüpfen und Anknüpfen an Stichwörter, Symbole oder dergleichen in den Sätzen tatsächlich zu einer Struktur verhalfen.
So ähnlich ging es wohl Vonnegut, der bei seiner Suche nach der richtigen Form für sein ureigenes persönliches Erleben auf diese „telepathic schizophrenic method" kam, die nun analysiert werden soll, denn bei aller – wahren oder gespielten – Bescheidenheit : Vonnegut macht geradezu Lust darauf, diese „short and jumbled and jangled novel'" zu entdröseln, stellt er uns doch vor die Frage: Ist Billy tatsächlich ein Zeitreisender oder sollten wir seine außerirdische Eskapade eher einem posttraumatischen Geisteszustand zuschreiben? Die Zeitreise, als das entscheidende inhaltliche Strukturelement, soll demnach als Erstes näher betrachtet werden.
Daher werden die Schülerinnen und Schüler im Anschluss nach dem Phänomen der „Zeitreise" in anderen Werken befragt:

> - Apart from *Slaughterhouse-Five,* do you know other stories of "time travel"?
> - How are they different from Billy Pilgrim's "jumps"?

Schülerinnen und Schüler können vielleicht einige ältere *Science-Fiction*-Titel nennen, z. B. *The Time Machine* von H.G. Wells, oder die Serien *The Time Tunnel,* einige *Star Trek-* (*Raumschiff Enterprise*) und *Stargate*-Episoden, o. Ä. Der Unterschied ist, dass in diesen Geschichten oder Filmen technische Mittel zur bewussten Zeitreise nötig sind.[1] Als Nächstes sollen

[1] Etwas anders ist dies in dem auch verfilmten Roman *Orlando* von Virginia Woolf oder den Filmen *Groundhog Day* (Und täglich grüßt das Murmeltier) oder *Apocalypse now.* Es ist allerdings nicht zu erwarten, dass diese bekannt sind.

die Schülerinnen und Schüler sich überlegen, wie es wäre, wie Billy – unfreiwillig – von der Zeit losgelöst zu sein. Der Schreibauftrag kann auch als Hausaufgabe gegeben oder als solche ausgearbeitet werden.

- Imagine what would it be like to be unstuck in time. Write a short story.

Aus dem zweiten Kapitel wird dann beschrieben, wie Billy die Zeitsprünge erlebt. Dazu soll der erste Abschnitt in eigenen Worten wiedergegeben und zusammengefasst werden, an der Tafel wird das Ergebnis gesichert:

- What does it mean when the narrator tells us: "Billy Pilgrim has become unstuck in time"? Describe this phenomenon (p. 23).

Billy Pilgrim has become unstuck in time

- It is like walking through doors entering different periods of his life.
- He has seen his birth and death.
- When he goes back through a door, he will be in another different time so he can never be sure where he will be next.
- He has no control over the process: he can neither determine when he will "jump", where to, or how often it will happen in a row.
- He is "spastic in time", so it is like having cramps or seizures: it is a kind of disease.
- The trips are very often uncomfortable, and he is frightened of their occurrence.
- He doesn't like it, because it is strenuous.

➞ Causes?

...[continued]

Es lässt sich aus dem Wissen um den Gesamtzusammenhang und mit Hilfe der *Reading Companions* zudem bestimmen, dass diese Zustände in der Realzeit kaum von Dauer sind bzw. dass Billy in der Wahrnehmung seiner Umgebung schläft. Die Vermutung, dass seine Zeitinkonsistenz mit der Entführung durch die Außerirdischen zu tun hat, kann ganz klar ausgeräumt werden:

- Where is Billy in "real time" when he is in a "time warp"?

  For the outside world, he appears to be asleep.

- Why is Billy "unstuck in time" after all? And when did it happen for the first time?

  We do not get a real reason but it is definitely pointed out to us that it is not due to his stay with the Tralfamadorians: "Billy says that he first came unstuck in time in 1944, long before his trip to Tralfamadore. The Tralfamadorians didn't have anything to do with his coming unstuck. [...] Billy first came unstuck while World War Two was in progress." (p. 30)

Die Ergebnissicherung wird als Ergänzung dem obigen Tafelbild angefügt:

- …
- ➞ Reason?
- It happened in WW II for the first time (1944).
- The Tralfamadorians have nothing to do with it.
- Speculations:
- Post-traumatic stress symptom
- …

4.1 Analysing the structure by detecting the time travel sequences

Ab dem dritten Kapitel werden kontinuierlich Zeitsprünge wiedergegeben, die den Roman strukturieren. Vonnegut hat sich selbst nicht anders zu helfen gewusst, als seine dadurch wirr werdende Konstruktion auf einer Tapete zu entwerfen (vgl. S. 62). Den *Personal Computer* gab es noch nicht. In einem zeitlich größer anzulegenden Projekt (2 Doppelstunden) sollen die Schülerinnen und Schüler alle Zeitsprünge anhand ihrer Markierungen im Text und den Notizen in ihren *Reading Companions* auffinden und die sich so ergebende Struktur auf ein Poster, oder authentischer auf eine Tapete, übertragen.
Zur Einstimmung werden die Schülerinnen und Schüler gefragt, wie sie das Herumspringen in der Geschichte empfinden:

- Is it fun to jump around, or does it make it hard to follow the story?

Sie sollen überlegen, wo man solchen non-linearen Strukturen sonst in der Kunst oder Musik begegnet. Zur nächsten Stunde könnte ein kurzer Schülervortrag ein solches Werk vorstellen und etwas zur Auflockerung der folgenden intensiven Textarbeitsphase beitragen.
Eine optische Anregung für die Arbeitsphase kann das Vonnegut-Bild mit der Tapete sein. Die Vorlage ***Copy 10, Travelling in time – instructions for analysing the structure, S. 62*** kann auf Folie kopiert werden, sodass praktischerweise gleich die Arbeitsanweisungen eingeblendet werden.
In arbeitsteiliger Gruppenarbeit (3 – 4 Schülerinnen und Schüler je Team) werden alle Kapitel nach Zeitreise-Passagen mit Hilfe der *Reading Companions* durchforstet. Die Schülerinnen und Schüler überlegen sich für ihre Kapitel eine schematische Darstellung. Am Ende werden alle Einzelkapitel in der Abfolge aufgehängt, gegebenenfalls auf eine Tapete übertragen und in einer Zusammenschau beurteilt.
Die Lösungen finden sich auf den Kopien im Anschluss an das Aufgabenblatt. Wenn keine Zeit für das Projekt ist, können diese alternativ zur Abwandlung der Strukturanalyse benutzt werden. Die Schülerinnen und Schüler sollen dann die Passagen auf ihre Richtigkeit und Vollständigkeit überprüfen und einen zusammenhängenden erklärenden Text zu den schematischen Darstellungen verfassen. Dazu werden fünf Gruppen gebildet. Jede Gruppe erhält je zwei Kapitel-Diagramme zur Bearbeitung (***Copy 11, Travelling in time – analysing the structure of Slaughterhouse-Five, S. 63***).

4.2 Project evaluation

Für die Auswertung der Kapitelstrukturanalysen ist noch einmal der Ausgangspunkt in Erinnerung zu rufen: Billy Pilgrim erzählt 1968 als wohlsituierter Veteran, dass ihm die Zeitreisen zum ersten Mal 1944 im Zweiten Weltkrieg passiert sind.
Im fünften Kapitel wird das bis dahin nachvollziehbare Springen unübersichtlicher, sodass der Erzähler sogar auktorial eingreift und eine Art „Reset" vornimmt: "Listen: Billy says he went to Dresden, Germany, on the day after his morphine night."(p. 136). Denn Billy erzählt nun nicht mehr das, was er im Krieg an Zeitreisen erlebt hat, sondern einzelne Episoden, die mehr lose Erinnerungen an Zeitreisen zu Geschehen im Krieg oder zu anderen Zeiten seines Lebens sind: "Billy Pilgrim **says now** that this really is the way he is going to die, too. As a time-traveler, he has seen his own death many times, has described it to a tape recorder..." (p. 140).
Mit Kapitel Fünf dreht sich die Perspektive. Die Zeitreise-Episoden werden von Billy Pilgrim nicht mehr als seine Erinnerungen aus der Perspektive des jungen Kriegsgefangenen erzählt, sondern aus seiner realen Zeit, 25 Jahre später. Alle Kriegsszenen sind nun Erinnerungen, die von Billy Pilgrim als Zeitreisen bezeichnet werden. Es ist die Rede von „Fore-seeings" (chapter 6–9) und davon, dass er träumt (ch. 9). Das macht skeptisch. Vonnegut sät den Verdacht, dass Billy Pilgrim nicht wirklich in der Zeit reist.
Der Anfang von Kapitel 7 ist bemerkenswert, denn es findet kein „flash" statt, kein Hinweis auf einen Zeitsprung, sondern der Erzähler tritt auktorial auf und erklärt den Zeitsprung vom gegenwärtigen Zeitpunkt aus als eine ganz normale Blende in die Zukunft: "Billy Pilgrim got onto a chartered airplane in Ilium 25 years later."(ch. 7; p. 156)
Die folgenden Erschließungsfragen sind relativ offen, um den Schülerinnen und Schülern die Möglichkeit zu geben, den erwähnten Perspektivenwandel ab dem 5. Kapitel selbst zu erkennen. Sollte dies nicht geleistet werden können, kann enger geführt werden, indem auf den Plakaten die Unterschiede gezeigt und fragend entwickelt werden.
Erschließungsfragen:

- Comment on the structure. Do you see a system?

Schülerinnen und Schüler sollten die relativ systematische Abfolge von Kriegssituation – Zeitreise bis Kapitel 5 erkennen, ab da die Veränderung bis hin zum Erzählperspektivenwechsel und der Vermischung von Zeitreise – Erinnerung – Vorsehung – Traum – Realität.

- Vonnegut told us that he designed the story on a wallpaper (as we did) – why then the chaos? Did he really mess it up, as he said of the book himself (cf. chapter 1)?

Die Schülerinnen und Schüler sollen erkennen, dass Vonnegut genau die richtige Form gefunden hat, denn er sagt ja, es gibt keine Art und Weise, keine Form, keine Möglichkeit, Massaker zu beschreiben. Die Struktur spiegelt genau das. Nach den traumatischen Erlebnissen gibt es nur eine solche Zerrissenheit, eine verzweifelte Verknüpfung der Erlebnisse, die ein Leben ausmachen, das von so einem existenziell bedrohlichen Erlebnis zerrissen wurde. Mit der bruchstückhaften Montage der Lebensfetzen wird ein Leben rekonstruiert, das seinen Sinn in diesen Erinnerungen und Erfahrungen (wieder) finden muss. Die flickenhafte Reparatur der Vergangenheit ist notwendig, um aus der Demütigung, der Traumatisierung herauszufinden und um weiterleben zu können, nachdem das Wertvollste, was das Leben ausmacht, die Menschenwürde, so erschüttert wurde.

Es kann plakativ an der Tafel festgehalten werden:

"There is no way to describe massacre."

...the only way of conveying this message is that "telepathic schizophrenic manner of tales of the planet Tralfamadore".

➡ The structure mirrors the fragmentation of life:

As the bombardment of Dresden has scattered the city into pieces, the patch-work-like novel is the only form of expressing the human condition thereafter and trying to mend the pieces.

Eine Zusammenfassung der Ergebnisse kann folgende Aspekte enthalten:

- After the Dresden horror, no form was adequate for conveying the author's emotions and experiences.
- The fragmented structure mirrors how war interrupts the life of a human being and leaves lives in tatters.
- By setting a frame with the first chapter which resembles a prologue, Vonnegut matches passages of his protagonist's life together into a patchwork, by first letting him drift from the battlefield and war to childhood and memories of private life and far off to the planet Tralfamadore by trips travelling in time.
- In the middle of the novel, in chapter five, when the interweaving of events threatens to get confusing, the method changes somewhat. The trips travelling in time are more and more substituted by forecasts and dreams.
- The author creates the impression of circularity and Billy Pilgrim being at the mercy of the meaninglessness of life.

Als Hausaufgabe und zur Vorbereitung der nächsten Unterrichtssequenz sollen die Schülerinnen und Schüler textgestützt erörtern, ob Billy Pilgrim tatsächlich ein Zeitreisender ist. Im Idealfall wird die Problematik der Glaubwürdigkeit erkannt und der Verdacht auf einen posttraumatischen Zustand geäußert:

- Does Billy Pilgrim really travel in time? Argue in favour or against the issue by referring to the text (focus on chapter 2).

Billy Pilgrim claims that he had become "unstuck in time", that is a person who does not live a normal linear chronology but instead moves in different episodes of his life at the same time as his present (ch. 2, p. 23). He ascertains that this phenomenon has nothing to do with his alien encounter and his abduction to the planet Tralfamadore (ch. 2, p. 30). Otherwise, one would have believed in a science fiction phenomenon, a kind of superpower due to the extraterrestrials. This conclusion would make a lot of sense, since the Tralfamadorians are creatures who have a special relationship to time. They are able to "see" the fourth dimension, that is they can see time and "they had many wonderful things to teach Earthlings, especially about time". So we may not wholly believe Billy denying the connection – if we believe in the "flying saucer" story at all. There is evidence that this event is a mere fantasy of a 46-year-old who has gone senile because of damage to his brain that was caused in the plane crash. This is one explanation Barbara, his daughter, offers (p. 28).

The interspersed comments of the author lead us to the idea that Billy might be trapped in a self-lie about his trips travelling in time. For example, the narrator points out that the assertions are uttered by Billy, but the way he lets Billy talk to the readers is most peculiar. First, he creates attention for Billy – as if a child has to be taken care of at its first performance in front of a terrifying audience: "Listen:..." Then he recounts Billy's statement. After that, he points out in a predominant extra line: "He says." (ch. 2, p. 23; further on cf. ch. 6: "Listen: Billy says he went to Dresden, Germany, on the day after his morphine night." p. 136; "Billy Pilgrim **says now** that this really is the way he is going to die, too." p. 141) This should make us sceptical about his credibility. And in fact, what comes next – especially the science fiction part – is hard to believe.
These hints lead us to a more realistic explanation of the trips travelling in time: Billy has suffered from such a lot of misery in his life that his account of travelling in time and "galactical zoo-life" might be the products of a diseased imagination – the results of the medical condition "post-traumatic stress".

Die Aufgabe kann eine Vorbereitung auf eine lebhafte Debatte über die Ursache für Billys Zeitreise-Phänomen sein. Sie bietet sich nach der Beschäftigung mit der Definition von einem Kriegstrauma an.

4.3 The time traveller – Billy Pilgrim's dislocation in life as post-war trauma

Die Diskussion um die Ursache für Billy Pilgrims Zeitreise ergibt sich aus der vorangegangenen Aufgabe. Die Vermutung, dass Billy Pilgrim an einer Geistesstörung aufgrund seiner traumatischen Erlebnisse in der Kindheit und besonders im Krieg durch die Bombardierung Dresdens leidet, soll mithilfe eines Sachtextes zum sogenannten PTSD (posttraumatic stress disorder)[1] erhärtet werden ***(Copy 12, Post-traumatic stress disorder, S. 69)***.
Nach der gemeinsamen Lektüre der Informationen kann die Aufgabe

- Do you consider Billy Pilgrim a victim of PTSD? Compare the indications given in the text with Billy's behaviour.

im Gespräch gelöst werden. Dazu können Kleingruppen mittels der Strukturposter, der *Reading Companions* und des Textes die im Sachtext genannten Symptome suchen und die PTSD-Hypothese mit Belegen erhärten. Das Ergebnis wird an der Tafel festgehalten:

[1] Deutsch: PTBS (Posttraumatische Belastungsstörung)

Is Billy Pilgrim a victim of PTSD (Post-traumatic stress disorder)?

Indications:

1. He "travels in time" and believes that he has been on the planet Tralfamadore where he was converted into a prophet of their philosophy.
(= intrusive fantasy/diseased imagination/loss of integrity and of personal identity)

2. His episodes travelling in time show scenes from his childhood that were significant.
   - His father exposed him to fear for his life:

   "sink or swim method"; darkness in the Carlsberg Caverns; standing close to the edge of the Canyon, wetting his pants out of fear
   - His mother bothered him with her false religiousness, e.g. she fixes a horrible cross to the wall of his room.

   (= childhood traumata: father-son-relationship/mother-son-relationship especially with respect to religion/religious conviction → emotional abuse)

3. The war experience:
   - He has witnessed and experienced abhorrent scenes in World War II as a POW.
   - He was shocked by the incineration of Dresden and the charred corpses.

4. Physical factors:
   - He has suffered from severe brain damage by the plane crash.
   - He has weeping fits for no apparent reason.

   (= physiological indications/medical cause)

5. The horrible death of his beloved wife Valencia
(= grief mixed with feelings of guilt)

Die These, dass Billy Pilgrim ein Opfer posttraumatischer Störungen ist, hat sich als sehr wahrscheinlich erwiesen. Die Frage liegt auf der Hand: Was hat Billy tatsächlich erlebt, das ihn zu dem „senile prophet of Tralfamadore" gemacht hat? Sein Leben weist drei Bereiche auf, die bruchstückhaft miteinander verwoben werden, wie die bisherige Beschäftigung mit der Struktur ergeben hat: seine Kriegserlebnisse, sein Privatleben besonders als Veteran und Optiker, sein Aufenthalt auf Tralfamadore. Dröselt man die Struktur auf, so wie die Projektarbeit es ermöglicht hat, so löst sich aus dem vermeintlichen Durcheinander je eine logische Geschichte. Um diese geht es in den nächsten Unterrichtssequenzen.
Eine Pro- und Contra-Debatte auf der Grundlage der Sachtextbearbeitung und der Spekulation über die Zeitreisen, wie sie sich aus der Strukturanalyse ergeben hat (s.o.) bildet einen handlungsorientierten, kommunikativ lebendigen Abschluss dieses *Components*.

Travelling in time – instructions for analysing the structure

- Gather in groups of 3–4 people. Work on your chapter.
- Use your reading companions and the book.
- Find all the passages where Billy makes a "time jump".
- What is the structure like according to these sequences? Draw a graph for your chapter.
- Present your graph on a big poster or – as Vonnegut did – on a piece of wallpaper!
- Hang all the posters up in a row and see what they look like!

Travelling in time – analysing the structure of *Slaughterhouse-Five*

Billy Pilgrim tells us the following in 1968:

1940s (and infancy)	1950s	1960s (and Tralfamadore)
Chapter 2		
1. It first happened in 1944: war – "through the full arc of his life": living through pre-birth, swimming lesson with father "sink-or-swim" (p. 43).	The time "jumps" 1., 2, … →	**2.** From the 1940s and boyhood, he travelled in time to 1965 (p. 44). 1965: he visits his mother at an old people's home. "Billy blinked in 1965, traveled to 1958" (p. 45).
	3. 1958: Little League team honour banquet for Robert (Ch.2, pp. 45–46). "Billy blinked in 1958 and travelled in time to 1961" (p. 46).	
		4. 1961: New Year's Eve and Billy's disgraceful behavior. He once and only once betrays his wife (p. 46).
1944: "Now somebody was shaking Billy awake […] He was back in World War Two again, behind the German lines" (p. 47).	The cheering went on, but its tone was altered as the hallucination gave way to time travel ("skating" into 1957) (p. 49).	
	5. Early afternoon in 1957 at a lectern in a Chinese restaurant in Ilium, N. Y., receiving a standing ovation as newly elected President of the Lions Club. He delivers a grand speech. (p. 49)	
1944: "And then he was back in the bed of the frozen creek again. Roland Weary was about to beat the living shit out of him" (p. 50).		
Chapter 3		
Billy went to sleep with his head on the shoulder of an unprotesting captain […] Billy traveled in time, opened his eyes, and found himself staring into the glass eyes of a jade green mechanical owl" (p. 55–56).		**6.** 1967: "Billy had fallen asleep while examining a female patient" through his optometrist apparatus (p. 57).

1940s (and infancy)	1950s	1960s (and Tralfamadore)
"Billy closed his eyes. When he opened them, he was back in World War Two again." (p. 58).		
7. "Billy's smile , as he came out of the shrubbery was at least as peculiar as Mona Lisa's, for **he was simultaneously on foot in Germany in 1944 and riding his Cadillac in 1967." (p. 58)**		
		8. 1967: he rides through Ilium's black ghetto to attend a Lions Club meeting on the war in Vietnam and have lunch as the past president; he is now "as rich as Croesus" and has weeping fits (pp. 59–63).
"He closed his eyes [...] He was still weeping, but he was back in Luxembourg again" (p. 63).		
First narrator's intrusion: "I was there, so was my old war buddy, Bernard V. O'Hare," (p. 67).		
"Somewhere in there [the boxcar] was Christmas. Billy P. nestled like a spoon"... (p. 71)		**9.** ... and "traveled in time to 1967 again – to the night he was kidnapped by a flying saucer from Tralfamadore" (p. 71).
Chapter 4		**Foreseeing:** his daughter's wedding night in 1967. Billy knows that he will be kidnapped by a flying saucer (p. 72).
		"The terrific acceleration of the saucer as it left Earth" dislodged him in time, sent him back to the war. "When he regained consciousness" ... (p. 77).
... "He was in a boxcar crossing Germany again" (p. 77).		
10. "The Americans clothes were meanwhile passing through poison gas" ... And Billy zoomed back in time to his infancy (p. 84). Around 1922: he was a baby who had just been bathed by his mother ... Billy gurgled and cooed. (pp. 84–85)	**11.** 1950s–60s: "And then he was a middle-aged optometrist again playing hacker's golf [...]. "He bent over to take the ball out of the cup [...] When he recovered, he wasn't on the golf course any more" (p. 85).	**12.** "He was strapped to a yellow contour chair in a white chamber aboard a flying saucer, which was bound for Tralfamadore" (p. 85).
Chapter 5		"Moments after that, the saucer entered a time warp, and Billy was flung back into his childhood." (p. 88)
13. 1934: he was 12 years old, quaking as he stood with his mother and father on Bright Angel Point, at the rim of Grand Canyon ... And Billy took a very short trip through time, made a peewee		

1940s (and infancy)	1950s	1960s (and Tralfamadore)
jump of only ten days … (p. 89). He is still 12 years old and still touring the West with his family. Billy is afraid of the dark and bats in Carlsbad Caverns where, again, his father made him go (pp. 89–90).		
"Billy went from total dark to total light, found himself back in the war, and back in the delousing station" (p. 90).		
Billy in his morphine dream: "Night came to the garden of the giraffes, and Billy Pilgrim slept without dreaming for a while, and then he traveled in time." (p. 99)		
14. Springtime 1948: "He woke up … in a ward for nonviolent mental patients in a veterans' hospital near Lake Placid, New York" (p. 99).		
15. "Billy fell asleep under his blanket. When he woke up again, he was tied to the bed in the hospital back in prison." (p. 105)		
"Billy traveled in time back to the veterans' hospital again" (p. 107). **16.** 1948: he is at the veterans' hospital again, where he is visited by his fiancée Valencia (p. 111). While they talk about the pattern for their silver cutlery, Billy travels in time (p. 111).		**17.** "And Billy traveled in time to the zoo on Tralfamadore. He was 44 years old, on display under a geodesic dome." (p. 111)
		On Tralfamadore, "shortly after he went to sleep that night, Billy traveled in time to another moment, which was quite nice" … (p. 118).
	18. His – quite nice – wedding night with Valencia (p. 118)	
	He "went into the darkness of the bathroom to take a leak. He groped for the light, realized as he felt the rough walls that"… (p. 123).	
19. … "he had traveled back to 1944, to the prison hospital again" (p. 123).		
Second narrator's intrusion: "That was I. That was me. That was the author of this book." (p. 125)		

1940s (and infancy)	1950s	1960s (and Tralfamadore)
"He came to the door of the little hospital by accident. He went through the door and" … (p. 126)	**20.** … "found himself honeymooning again, going from the bathroom back to bed…. Billy and Valencia nestled like spoons" … (p. 126).	
21. … and "Billy traveled in time back … to the train ride he had taken in 1944 – from manoeuvres in South Carolina to his father's funeral in Ilium. He hadn't seen Europe or combat yet" (p. 126).		
Billy sleeps in the dining car and is …		
… in 1944 at the hospital: he is woken up at 3 o'clock in the morning by Lazzaro's arrival… Billy falls asleep during Campbell's speech (p. 131).		**22.** … Billy P. woke up as a widower in his empty home in Ilium. His daughter Barbara was reproaching him for writing ridiculous letters. It was 1968 again …
		23. "When Barbara left, slamming the door behind her, Billy traveled in time to the zoo on Tralfamadore again" (p. 132).
		"A mate had just been brought to him from Earth. She was Montana Wildhack" … (p. 132).
		"And Billy traveled in time from the delightful bed to a bed in 1968" (p. 134).
		It was his bed in Ilium, and the electric blanket was turned up high. He was drenched in sweat … (p. 134).
Chapter 6		

Auctorial narration:
Listen: Billy says he went to Dresden, Germany, on the day after his morphine night. =
Set back to January 1945 by the narrator (p. 136). Billy Pilgrim **says now** that this really is the way he is going to die, too. As a time traveller, he has seen his own death many times and has recorded it on a tape recorder: "I, Billy Pilgrim […] will die, have died, and always will die on February thirteenth, 1976". (p. 141) – in the description of his death he swings back into life again, all the way back to an hour after his life was threatened by Lazzaro – in 1945 (p. 143).

Third narrator's intrusion: "Somebody behind him in the boxcar said, 'Oz'. That was I. That was me …" (p. 148).		
Foreseeing: "Billy, with his memories of the future, knew that Dresden would be smashed to smithereens" … (p. 150).		

1940s (and infancy)	1950s	1960s (and Tralfamadore)
Chapter 7	No indication of travelling in time – auctorial information that the following **events take place 25 years later**: Billy Pilgrim got onto a chartered airplane in Ilium 25 years later. He knew it was going to crash …	
		Foreseeing: he knew the plane was going to crash (p. 154).
		Billy, knowing the plane was going to crash fairly soon, closed his eyes and travelled in time back to 1944 (p. 156).
24. 1944: "He was back in the forest in Luxembourg again – with the Three Musketeers" (p. 156).		
		25. On the plane: the barbershop quartet was singing … when the plane smacked into the top of Sugarbush Mountain in Vermont. Everybody was killed but Billy (p. 156).
		"He was taken to a small private hospital … Billy was unconscious for two days … The true things were time-travel" (p. 157).
26. One of the true things was his first evening in the slaughterhouse … (p. 157). Another true thing that Billy saw while he was unconscious in Vermont was the work … in Dresden (p. 159).		
Chapter 8		
1945 (Feb. 11): Howard W Campbell, Jr. visits the slaughterhouse to recruit men for the Free American Corps (p. 162). Foreseeing: "It was the next night that about 130 000 people in Dresden would die" (p. 165).		
1945: Billy dozed in the meat locker … He found himself engaged again … (p. 165).		**27.** 1968: … in the argument with his daughter with which this tale began (p. 165).
		Memory in 1968: "Billy thought hard about the effect the quartet had had on him … **He did not travel in time … He remembered it shimmeringly – as follows:** He was down in the meat locker on **the night Dresden was destroyed.**" (p. 177)

1940s (and infancy)	1950s	1960s (and Tralfamadore)
		Memory in 1968 of Tralfamadore: Montana wants him to tell a story. Billy tells her about the destruction of Dresden (pp. 178–181).
Chapter 9	No indication of leaving the memory – a new episode is opened by the narrator: here is how Billy Pilgrim lost his wife, Valencia (p. 182).	
	1968: he was unconscious in hospital in Vermont after the airplane crash … Valencia was hysterical… One hour later she was dead. … Billy knew nothing about it. He **dreamed on, and travelled in time and so forth** (pp. 182–183). When Barbara and Robert come to visit him, he is ten years removed, back in 1958.	
	28. 1958: "He was examining the eyes of a young male Mongolian idiot" … (pp. 188–189)	
29. 1938: "Billy traveled in time to when he was sixteen years old, in the waiting room of a doctor." (p. 189)		
		30. 1968: "Billy Pilgrim opened his eyes in the hospital of Vermont, did not know where he was" (p. 189). His roommate is Prof. Rumfoord.
31. Billy closed his eyes, travelled in time to a May afternoon, two days after the end of the Second World War in Europe (p. 193).		
1945: Billy and five other Americans were riding … a wagon … They were going back to the slaughterhouse for souvenirs of the war (p. 194).		
		32. "Billy traveled in time back to the hospital in Vermont … Rumfoord was reluctantly becoming interested in Billy"… (p. 197).
		"He was gently expelled from the studio … He went back to his hotel room … and he went to sleep. He traveled in time back to Tralfamadore" (pp. 206–207).

Chapter 10

No travelling in time – instead a rather linear structure:
The narrator tells the reader about tragic deaths. He talks about what Billy learnt on Tralfamadore (p. 211).
He remembers his trip back to Dresden with O'Hare and supposes that Billy Pilgrim was going back to Dresden in 1945, where he and O'Hare had been. He reports on Billy's work as a grave-digger preparing the first "corpse mine" in Dresden. Edgar Derby was executed for stealing a teapot. One day, Billy and the others found the door unlocked; the war was over in Europe. Springtime had come (pp. 211–215).

Post-traumatic stress disorder (PTSD)

Trauma: (psychology) a mental condition caused by severe shock, especially when the harmful effects last for a long time (*OALD*)

Posttraumatic stress disorder (PTSD) is a severe anxiety disorder that can develop after exposure to any event that results in psychological trauma. This event may involve the threat of death to oneself or to someone else, or to one's own or someone else's physical, sexual, or psychological integrity, overwhelming the individual's ability to cope. As an effect of psychological trauma, PTSD is less frequent and more enduring than the more commonly seen post traumatic stress (also known as acute stress response). Diagnostic symptoms for PTSD include re-experiencing the original trauma(s) through flashbacks or nightmares, avoidance of stimuli associated with the trauma, and increased arousal – such as difficulty falling or staying asleep, anger, and hyper-vigilance. Formal diagnostic criteria require that the symptoms last more than one month and cause significant impairment in social, occupational, or other important areas of functioning.
PTSD is believed to be caused by experiencing any of a wide range of events which produces intense negative feelings of „fear, helplessness or horror" in the observer or participant. Sources of such feelings may include (but are not limited to):

- experiencing or witnessing childhood or adult physical, emotional, or sexual abuse; experiencing or witnessing physical assault, adult experiences of sexual assault, accidents, drug addiction, illnesses, or medical complications;
- employment in occupations exposed to war (such as soldiers) or disaster (such as emergency service workers);
- receiving a diagnosis of a life-threatening illness.

Children or adults may develop PTSD symptoms by experiencing bullying or mobbing. It has been shown that the intrusive memories, such as flashbacks, nightmares, and the memories themselves, are greater contributors to the biological and psychological dimensions of PTSD than the event itself. These intrusive memories are mainly characterized by sensory episodes, rather than thoughts. People with PTSD have intrusive re-experiences of traumatic events, in which awareness of context and time is lost. These episodes aggravate and maintain PTSD symptoms, since the individual re-experiences trauma as if it was happening in the present moment.

Based on: Wikipedia, the free encyclopedia (Aufruf: 3.3.2013)

exposure to *here*: contact with

integrity *here*: the state of being whole and not divided

arousal excitement

hyper-vigilance übersteigerte Wachsamkeit

impairment damage; disability

assault physical attack

intrusive *sich aufdrängend*

to aggravate *here:* to make worse

- Do you consider Billy Pilgrim a victim of PTSD? Compare the indications given in the text with Billy's behaviour.

Component 5

Billy Pilgrim and the war

Aus der verzwickten Romanstruktur lassen sich eigentlich drei *plots* herauslösen, die Billys Leben als Kriegsdienstleistenden, Ehemann und erfolgreichen Optiker und Gefangenen von Außerirdischen darstellen. Dabei ist der Dreh- und Angelpunkt des Romans die katastrophale Bombardierung Dresdens, wenn diese auch erst in den letzten Kapiteln konkret wird. In nahezu jedem Kapitel erinnert sich Billy schmerzhaft an die Zeit als POW in dem Schlachthaus in Dresden. Wie hat Billy diese Zeit tatsächlich erlebt?

Mit der CD können die ersten eindrucksvollen Kriegserlebnisse, die Billys erste Zeitreise auslösten, in Erinnerung gebracht werden. Die Schülerinnen und Schüler lesen nach Erteilung der Arbeitsaufträge folgende Ausschnitte des 2. Kapitels mit, oder man gestaltet diese Sequenz als reine Höraufgabe und lässt die Bücher geschlossen:

CD 1 Track 5 (ganz) – fortsetzen mit	Text on p. 30 (lower middle): "And so on. Billy says that he first came unstuck …"
CD 1 Track 6 (- 08.40) – unterbrechen und fortsetzen mit	up to the end of the text on p. 44 (first paragraph): "… Billy resented that" – skip the text up to
CD 2 Track 1 – Idealstart bei 02:46 bis zum Ende spielen	p. 47: "Now somebody was shaking Billy awake" to the end

Die Höraufträge werden vor der Einspielung an der Tafel oder auf dem OHP notiert. Es sollen Stichworte angefertigt werden.

Billy Pilgrim and the war

1. Why did Billy go to war?
2. What kind of "soldier" is he?
3. How did he meet Roland Weary?
4. What kind of soldier is Roland?
5. What is Billy's relationship with him like?

Lösungen:

1. Why did Billy go to war?

   He was not a voluntary soldier. He was ordered overseas after a training season in South Carolina as a valet to a priest and an assistant to a chaplain.

2. What kind of "soldier" is he?

   He is a figure of fun in the American Army, powerless to harm the enemy or to help friends; there are no promotions or medals in sight. He has no helmet, no overcoat, no weapon, and no boots. He unnerves the others by singing hymns and praying. He is only 21 years old but is already going bald. He didn't look like a soldier at all. He looked like a "filthy flamingo" (p. 33).

3. How did he meet Roland Weary?

He meets Roland Weary "by accident". Billy got lost behind the German lines like Weary and his three scouts.

4. What kind of soldier is he?

Weary dreams of being the perfect soldier. He is 18 years old and "had fat to burn". He is a weapon fetishist and overloaded with weapons. He wears the right outfit for combat in winter as an anti-tank gunner. He is "clumsy and dense, coarse and brutal". His mindset is that of a practical person despising intellectuals like Billy, preferring his own personal wisdom, "There's more to life than what you read in books" (p. 38). He is brave in order to be honoured. He fantasizes about being part of the "Three Musketeers", as he calls his scouts (pp. 42–43).

5. What is Billy's relationship with him like?

Billy accepts him as the leader. He is, at the same time, amazed and repulsed by Weary's tales about his father, who had taught Weary to love weapons, torture instruments, and other perverse things. He tries to avoid too much conversation with Weary who is fairly talkative and imagines himself to be as brave and strong as the Three Musketeers. He saves Billy's life, so Billy is grateful but he does not really like the man.

Eine schriftliche Ausgestaltung der Begegnung zwischen Billy Pilgrim and Roland Weary soll den starken Kontrast zwischen dem Berufssoldaten und dem untauglichen Zwangsrekrutierten gut erfassen.
Dazu sollen sich die Schülerinnen und Schüler zunächst kreativ mit den beiden Charakteren beschäftigen. Sie könnten die beiden zeichnen, in die Rolle der jeweiligen Person schlüpfen, oder als der jeweils andere einander beurteilen. Eine künstlerische Umsetzung könnte eingefordert werden:

Create an illustration for the chapter showing both Billy and Roland. Take care to show their differences in appearance.

Die szenische Umsetzung besonders der letzten Situation, in der Weary zum Stoß mit dem Stiefel ansetzt, könnte in ein Standbild umgesetzt werden. Die Schülerinnen und Schüler sollen sich mögliche „freezes" oder „sculpts" aus dem Kapitel überlegen.
Dabei sollen die agierenden Schülerinnen und Schüler nach den Gefühlen und Gedanken der jeweiligen Romanfigur, aber unbedingt auch nach ihren eigenen Gefühlen bei der Darstellung dieser heftigen Situation gefragt werden. Entweder lässt man mehrere Gruppen untereinander die Szene entwickeln, oder man arbeitet mit der Klasse unter Anleitung einzelner „sculptors" so lange mit willigen DarstellerInnen, bis alle mit dem Bild zufrieden sind:

Let's have a freeze frame from that chapter. Choose a scene and perform it.

Daran kann sich eine weitere Frage anschließen:

Which character would you rather be in such a bad situation?

Das ist der Impuls für die Charakteranalyse, die zunächst wieder über die Identifizierung mit den Romanfiguren geschehen kann:

> Pretend you are either Billy or Roland. Describe the other one from your point of view.

Um eine ausgewogene Menge an "Billys" und "Rolands" zu erzeugen, kann man entweder die Gruppe zweiteilen, oder – arbeitsaufwändiger – vorgefertigte Karten mit den Namen austeilen. Die Charakterisierung wird zunächst schriftlich erarbeitet. Dies kann auch als Hausaufgabe vorbereitet werden.

5.1 Soldiers – Billy Pilgrim and Roland Weary

Die schriftlichen Charakterisierungen können dialogisch vorgetragen werden. Je eine Schülerin oder ein Schüler äußert sich zu der jeweiligen anderen Person. Die anderen Schülerinnen und Schüler beurteilen anschließend die Darbietungen. Dabei sollen sie ein *feedback* darüber geben, inwieweit die Beschreibungen mit dem Text und dem Charakter der Person übereinstimmen.[1] Die Vorträge werden dann für einen Vergleich ausgewertet, der an der Tafel oder am OHP gesichert wird:

Billy Pilgrim and Roland Weary and their appearances as soldiers (pp. 30–45)	
Billy Pilgrim	Roland Weary
• a chaplain's assistant and a valet to a preacher • a figure of fun in the American Army • powerless to harm the enemy or to help friends • He had no friends in the army. • no promotions or medals in sight • He bears no arms. • He is detested by the others because of his "meek faith in loving Jesus" (p. 31). • He was ordered overseas. • He is ready for death. • He is preposterous: no helmet, no overcoat, no weapons, and no boots • civilian clothes • bobbing way of walking because of lost heel • the only one with a beard partly white Only 21 years old but already going bald • crimson face → He didn't look like a soldier at all. He looked like a filthy flamingo (p. 33). • He wanted to quit (p. 34).	• an antitank gunner • clumsy and dense • He uses rude language ("motherfucker"; p. 34). • He beats up people who think they are his friends. • Two scouts are his companions. He calls the three of them "The Three Musketeers". • He had no friends at home. • heavily armed: colt and knife • He is stupid, fat, mean, and likes to beat people up. • He had every piece of equipment he had ever been issued ... Helmet ... He had a dirty picture of a woman. (pp. 39–40) • He is only 18 years old. → He looked like Tweedledum or Tweedledee, all bundled up for battle. • He had so much energy ... he began to suspect [...] that he was the leader (p. 41) = he enjoys the war

[1] Die Evaluation kann mit *feedback-worksheets* für die Zuschauenden noch fruchtbarer gemacht werden. Eine Vorlage für eine *observer card* findet man z. B. in *Method Guide.* Kreative Methoden für den Englischunterricht in der Oberstufe, A. Peschel und K. Schallhorn. Schöningh, Paderborn 2004, p. 75.

Billy Pilgrim	Roland Weary
• He was skinny (p. 41).	• He was short and thick (p. 39). • He had fat to burn. He was a roaring furnace under all his layers of wool ... (p. 41). • He had no sense of danger (p. 41). • He conceals his baby face (p. 41).
Conclusion:	
→ He is a defeatist and a weakling. → not fit for war	→ He is a professional soldier with an exaggerated penchant for violence. → superfit for war

Billy Pilgrim und Roland Weary sind grundverschieden. Billy ist eindeutig ungeeignet für den Krieg, Roland dagegen eine Kampfmaschine. Wieso hat Vonnegut eigentlich nicht Roland Weary, die starke Persönlichkeit, zu seinem Romanhelden gemacht? Die Schülerinnen und Schüler sollen die Frage in Partnerarbeit kurz besprechen. Die Ideen werden dann im Plenum gesammelt und kommentiert.

Aus dieser Diskussion kann sich die Folgefrage ergeben: Wie steht es tatsächlich mit den soldatischen Tugenden der Tapferkeit und Heldenhaftigkeit? Ist Roland auch hier Billy überlegen? Hierzu sollen die Schülerinnen und Schüler Stellung nehmen, nachdem sie ihre Aufzeichnungen in den *Reading Companions* oder ihre bei der Vorbereitung angefertigten Unterstreichungen zu Kapitel drei und vier überfliegen und nach geeigneten Informationen scannen:

> Which character is braver? Which character is more heroic? Use your preparation material (reading companions, bookmarks and so on) to answer.

Es wird erwartet, dass die Schülerinnen und Schüler erkennen, dass Roland, obwohl er sich wie ein Führer und Held fühlt, nicht die edlen Tugenden eines solchen erfüllt. Er rettet zwar Billy das Leben, aber er tut es, um heroisch zu wirken. Egoismus ist kein edler Grund für Tapferkeit. Er verfolgt die fixe Idee, als Held nach Hause zu kommen. Sein Mut und seine Tapferkeit beruhen auf diesem übersteigerten Selbstbild, das schnell zerfällt, als die beiden Scouts neben ihm erschossen werden. („And Weary, bug-eyed with terror, was being disarmed", ch. 3, p. 54). Er ist in Wirklichkeit auch kein guter Soldat. Wie Billy ist er neu. Auch er ist als Ersatz an die Front gekommen. Weil er einen unbeherrschten Schuss abfeuerte, verfehlte er das Ziel und brachte sogar den Feind, die Deutschen, auf die Spur des Geschützverstecks (ch. 2, p. 34).

So gesehen ist er ein Versager hinter seiner waffenklirrenden Fassade. Seine Entwaffnung wird daher auch sehr detailliert beschrieben und ist eine ironische Demontage des bulligen Kämpfers. Er wird auf Billys Ebene der Lächerlichkeit reduziert, indem seine Kleidung zerrissen wird und z. B. die Knöpfe wie Popkorn davonfliegen ("Brass buttons flew like popcorn", ch. 3, p. 54). Es bleibt nichts Martialisches mehr. Auch seine Stiefel muss er abgeben, ausgerechnet an den engelhaften, schmächtigen blonden deutschen Jungen. Nicht allein dadurch gedemütigt, bricht seine stolze, prahlerische Haltung unter den Schmerzen beim Laufen auf den wunden Füßen zusammen. Er ist genauso beklagenswert wie die Witzfigur Billy, mit der er die „fools' parade" anführt (ch. 3, p. 58). Die Verhöhnung geht sogar noch weiter. Auf dem Fußmarsch wird er von einem deutschen Soldaten, der den Sieg auf einem Panzer sitzend mit Alkohol und Blutwurst feiert, übel bespuckt (ch. 3, 64–65).

Billy ist nicht tapfer. Er will sogar aufgeben und sterben. Alles ist ihm egal. Im Sinne eines klassischen Heroen ist er das blanke Gegenteil. Er würde nicht einmal für sich selbst kämpfen.: "He wouldn't do anything to save himself. He wanted to quit. He was cold, hungry, embarrassed, incompetent." (ch.2, p. 34)

Als Hausaufgabe soll Roland Wearys Biografie verfasst werden:

Write Roland Weary's biography (use ch. 2–4).

Roland Weary

Die Anfertigung der Biografie von Roland Weary liefert die Grundlage für eine *hot seat activity*[1], bei der Roland Weary sein Verhalten gegenüber Billy erklären soll. Wieso war er ausgerastet und wollte dem am Boden liegenden Billy mit dem Stiefel ins Gesicht treten? Der oder die Spielende sollte so befragt werden oder so in die Enge getrieben werden, dass er oder sie die Schuld für sein aggressives Verhalten in der Kindheit und besonders der Rolle des Vaters sieht. Sein sadistisches Wesen muss verteidigt werden. Die Rolle eignet sich besonders für sprachlich recht sichere und aktive Schülerinnen und Schüler.
Eine Schülerin oder ein Schüler wird gebeten, die Rolle des Roland Weary auf dem *hot seat* einzunehmen. Die anderen Schülerinnen und Schüler erhalten folgende Anweisung:

Ask Roland Weary anything you want to know from him and especially about his behaviour towards Billy Pilgrim. Make sure you obtain complete sentences for answers and try to find out the truth behind Roland's rudeness.

Nach der Fragerunde sollte der oder die Spielende zuerst Gelegenheit erhalten, ihr Befinden in der Rolle zu reflektieren und dann ein *feedback* zu der spielerischen, inhaltlichen und sprachlichen Leistung vonseiten der anderen Schülerinnen und Schüler und der Lehrkraft erhalten.

Die Betrachtung Roland Wearys als Gegenbild zu Billy Pilgrim soll mit der Frage nach dessen Bedeutung für Billy abgeschlossen werden. Diese soll schriftlich in Stillarbeit oder als Hausaufgabe erfolgen. Folgende Aspekte sollten dabei erwähnt werden:

What does Roland Weary mean to Billy Pilgrim?

- Roland saves his life several times (p. 34).
- He is astonishing for Billy in terms of his rude behaviour and language (p. 34).
- He is cruel to Billy and keeps him alive by this (p. 34).
- He reveals human abysses to Billy which he had never known and which the narrator describes as a pattern with Roland who entered into "a crazy, sexy, murderous relationship with people he eventually beat up" (ch. 3, p. 59).
- Billy learns about sadism (torture with ant-heap, Iron Maiden) and fetishism (the pony photograph).
- When Roland wants to try out his "father's present" on Billy, he is close to become a part of Roland's perverse games (the spiked ring, p. 37).
- When Roland is left by his "Musketeers" (the scouts), he blames Billy for the breaking up of his "fighting organization" and Billy is almost killed by him (cf. the boot kick, p. 51).

[1] Mehr zur Organisation und Durchführung einer *hot seat activity* siehe in *Method Guide*, Kreative Methoden für den Englischunterricht in der Oberstufe, A. Peschel und K. Schallhorn. Schöningh, Paderborn, 2004.

- Billy will finally be killed because of Weary: Weary will take revenge on him. Billy is to blame for the loss of the scout friends and his boots. Because of this, Roland hurts his feet so badly that he finally dies of gangrene. His last words are a curse of revenge to be carried out by his then friend Lazzaro (ch. 4, pp. 79–80). Lazzaro will avenge Weary by fulfilling his wish to have Billy killed one day (ch. 5 p. 92).

5.2 Dresden

Rolands Bedeutung für Billy wurde von den Schülerinnen und Schüler schriftlich erarbeitet (siehe oben). Sie erhalten Gelegenheit, ihre Texte untereinander auszutauschen und zu besprechen. Nach gemeinsamer Überarbeitung kann eine Arbeit laut vorgelesen und kommentiert werden.

On the way to Dresden

Roland wurde bei der Verladung in die Zugabteile von Billy getrennt. Er hat den Zugtransport nach Dresden nicht überlebt. Was hat Billy auf dem Weg nach Dresden erlebt?
In arbeitsteiliger Gruppenarbeit sollen Billys Erlebnisse nachgezeichnet werden. Es ist eine Doppelstunde zu veranschlagen, wenn die Präsentation der Ergebnisse im Anschluss an die Arbeitsphase erfolgen soll. Jede Gruppe wird mindestens eine halbe Stunde für die Erarbeitung benötigen. Für die Präsentation erhält jede Gruppe eine Folie. Die Schreibenden sollten nicht die Vortragenden sein. Die Gruppen sollten einen *time-guard*, einen *writer* und einen *speaker* vorab bestimmen.
Zur Veranschaulichung des Weges kann nochmals die Karte (***Copy 6, The war locations, S. 45***) auf Folie präsentiert werden. Die angegebenen Textstellen helfen den Schülerinnen und Schülern, die entsprechenden Stellen im Text schnell zu finden, ansonsten können sie sich an den Aufzeichnungen in ihren *Reading Companions* orientieren oder ihren Unterstreichungen:

Give an account of what Billy Pilgrim experiences on the way to Dresden.

Die ***group tasks (Copy 13, S. 86)*** können kopiert und in die Gruppen hineingegeben werden. Vor der Arbeitsphase sollten die Aufgaben jedoch zunächst von allen gemeinsam gelesen werden, damit die Schülerinnen und Schüler eine Orientierung über das jeweilige Tun der anderen und ihren Bereich erhalten. Dazu kann das Arbeitsblatt zusätzlich auf Folie präsentiert werden.

Erwartete Ergebnisse:

Group 1: The prisoners' march:
- Weary and Billy do not have appropriate shoes for the long walk.
- They are taken to a stone cottage, a collecting point. Billy falls asleep there.
- The march goes on: the Americans form a fools' parade on the road (p. 58).
- A photographer with a Leica takes pictures of their feet to prove that the Americans are miserably equipped. To make the picture more vivid, Billy is thrown into the shrubbery.
- The march with a lot of other prisoners continues (p. 63).
- Billy sees St. Elmo's fire around the heads of his companions and captors.
- Weary is crying with pain; his feet are bleeding badly (p. 64).
- More and more American prisoners join the march. "Through the valley flowed a Mississippi of humiliated Americans" (p. 64).
- German reserves were rushing to the front on the other side of the road. They are celebrating, and one soldier spits on the Americans and hits Weary.

- "Billy found the afternoon stingingly exciting. There was so much to see – dragon's teeth, killing machines, corpses with bare feet that were blue and ivory" (p. 65).
- Finally, they reach Germany and a railroad yard where many boxcars are waiting for them.

Group 2: What happens on the boxcar ride?
- Billy is packed into a boxcar with many other privates. He and Weary are separated.
- Billy stands by one of the ventilators at the corner of the car where he can peep outside and see what the Germans are doing.
- The others are very young except for a hobo who is crammed against Billy.
- Billy watches as the Germans open another boxcar that is like heaven, the rolling home for the guards.
- The four guards go inside, still not paying attention to a man who has died in one of the other cars. It is Wild Bob (p. 68).
- Billy's train does not move for two days (p. 69).
- The car is kept locked: "each car became a single organism which ate and drank and excreted through its ventilators" (p. 70).
- Helmets are used as toilets, and Billy serves as dumper.
- The prisoners organize themselves, sharing food, standing, or lying down in turns.
- Then the train moves eastward at Christmas. Billy travels in time to the night when he got kidnapped by the Tralfamadorians (p. 71).

Group 3: What was it like for the prisoners and their guards to be in the boxcar? and Part 1 – What happens in the prison camp?
- The car was going at about two miles an hour, and Billy found it good to sleep. It seemed that with each "click" a year was going by (p. 77).
- The train often stops to let other trains pass or leave a few cars at prisons.
- Billy concentrates on making himself "ghostlike" in order not to disturb the others.
- The others hate him because he is kicking around in his sleep and whimpering. "Everybody told Billy to keep the hell away" (p. 79).
- So Billy has to sleep standing up or not at all.
- Food has stopped coming in and it is getting colder.
- On the ninth day, the hobo and Roland Weary die.
- Everybody hears Weary cursing Billy for killing him and that he should be avenged.
- On the tenth night, the door is opened. Billy is released like "Jesus from the cross" (p. 80).
- Billy is ill.
- They reach a prison that was an extermination camp for Russian prisoners.
- Billy and the others are provided with overcoats from prisoners that had died. Billy gets a funny-looking civilian coat (pp. 81–82).
- Billy blacks out as he has walked through gate after gate, but then he manages to undress as he is told in order to be examined. He meets Edgar Derby in the delousing shower (p. 84).
- Billy also meets Lazzaro.
- Billy "zooms back in time to his infancy" (pp. 84–85).

Group 4: Part 2 – What happens in the prison camp?
- Billy gets his clothes back. The coat is much too small, full of bullet holes, and he tears it apart to a vest: "The Germans found him to be one of the most screamingly funny things they had seen in all of World War Two. They laughed and laughed" (p. 90).
- Billy is made the pivot of a parade.
- Their names are documented. Billy gets a number and an iron dog tag.
- The American families were informed about their imprisonment after two days (p. 92).
- Lazzaro suffers from stomach ache and does not think of vengeance.

- In front of a shed, the parade is stopped and 50 Englishmen march out singing joyfully in welcome.
- They had already been imprisoned for four years and lived very comfortably due to a "clerical error" that had caused the Red Cross to ship them 500 care parcels every month instead of 50. They lived in "peace" with the Germans and enjoyed their privileges. They had prepared a welcome "party" for the Americans.
- They give the Americans presents like candles and soap – made of human fat, which they did not know (p. 96) – and put on a show of the musical "Cinderella" for them.
- Billy catches fire at the glowing stove while watching.
- Billy passes out.
- Billy is taken to the six-bed hospital. He has a dream about giraffes while under morphine and travels in time to his stay at the veterans' hospital at Lake Placid (p. 99).
- Derby and the Englishman who cares for Billy talk about the war as a "Children's crusade" and how the Americans got caught by the Germans (pp. 106–107).
- Bill, still affected by his time travelling and the morphine, leaves the bed in order to urinate outside. There, he sees a friendly Russian soldier which makes him contemplate life (p. 124).
- In the middle of the night, he awakes through cries from the latrine where the other Americans are because they could not keep the rich food in (p. 125).
- "Billy reeled away from his vision of Hell." He travels in time to his honeymoon with Valencia (p. 126).

Group 5: Why is Howard Campbell cited in the prison camp and what is going on there?

- The Englishmen despise the Americans. They think them even worse than the Russians (p. 127).
- A German major apologizes to the Englishmen for the inconvenience caused to them by the Americans and reads from a monograph published by the German Association of Prison Officials. It is a report on the behaviour of American prisoners of war in Germany written by Howard W. Campbell, Jr.
- Campbell had been a fairly well-known playwright, a native of Schenectady, New York. He had the highest IQ of all the war criminals (p. 129) and later on hung himself before his trial (p. 128).
- In his report on the Americans' bad behaviour, lack of decency, self-centredness and lack of love for their fellow men, he comes to the conclusion that the Americans were known everywhere to be the most self-pitying, least fraternal, and dirtiest of all prisoners of war. They were incapable of concerted action, despised any leader from among their own number, refused to follow or even listen to him because they did not accept orders by their likes (p. 131).
- Billy is somehow magically drawn towards his coat hanging on the wall behind him. He feels two small lumps hidden in the lining. He does not check what they are but believes in them as good luck charms since he feels a radiation like animal magnetism coming from them (p. 137).
- Outside, new latrines are dug out.
- Lazzaro quarrels with an Englishman who only wants to help. He calls revenge the sweetest thing of all (p. 138).
- Lazzaro tells the horror story about a dog he tormented to death (p. 139).
- Lazzaro talks about his plan to kill the one who had caused Weary's death and warns Billy to take care in future when he hears his door bell ring. One day, it will be his murderer sent by Lazzaro (p. 141). As a time traveller, Billy knows that already.
- The Englishmen lecture on hygiene and how to survive in the camp (p. 145).
- Their departure for Dresden is announced.
- Edgar Derby is elected leader of the American POWs (p. 146).

Als schriftliche Hausaufgabe werden Lazzaro und Derby zur „Wahl" vergeben:

Choose one of the characters, either Paul Lazzaro or Edgar Derby, in order to describe them and their relationship to Billy Pilgrim and Roland Weary.

The prisoners of war

Die vorbereitete Beschreibung der neuen Bekanntschaften von Billy, Paul Lazzaro und Edgar Derby dienen neben deren Charakterisierung dazu, die Beziehung der Personen, die als Kriegsgefangene bis zum Kriegsende zusammenleben, herauszuarbeiten.

Zunächst soll die Identität von Paul Lazzaro und Edgar Derby geklärt werden. Edgar Derby wurde bereits im ersten Kapitel als der eigentliche tragische Held vorgestellt, hier nun ist sein Auftritt als der väterliche „Kümmerer". Das Wesentliche zu seiner Person und zu Paul Lazzaro als Romanfigur kann mit den Ausführungen unter *Characters* (S. 10) abgeglichen werden.

Die Beziehungen zwischen den vier Kriegsgefangenen lassen sich in einem Trapezdiagramm als Resümee aus den Hausarbeiten und dem Unterrichtsgespräch darstellen:

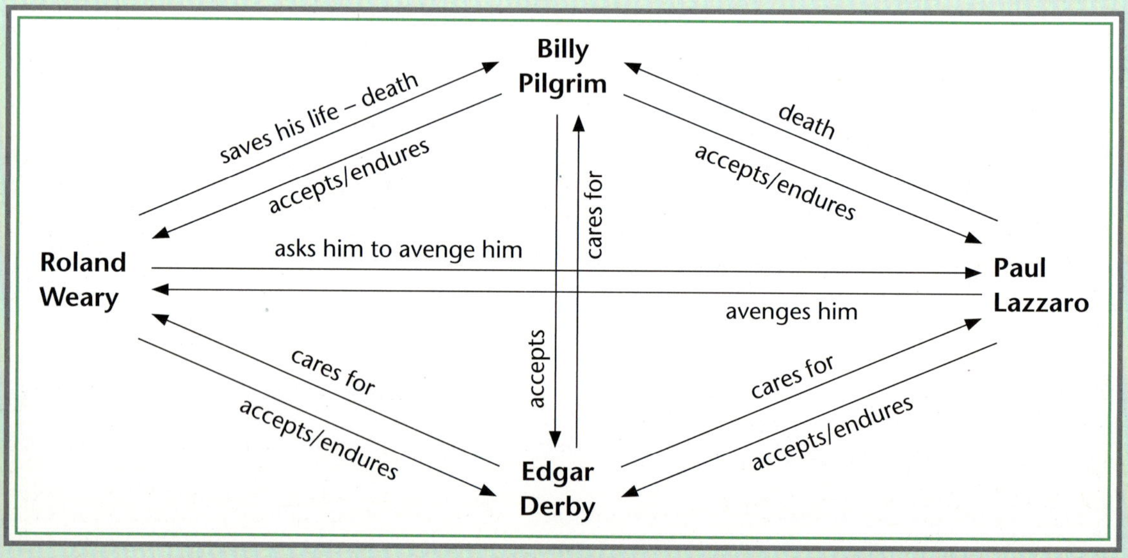

Erläuterung der Abbildung:
Billy Pilgrim – Roland Weary: Billy accepts/endures Weary as the leader behind the German lines. Weary saves his life but he will cause his death in 1976 with Lazzaro's help. Weary blames Billy Pilgrim for his dying because of gangrene.
Billy Pilgrim – Paul Lazzaro: Billy accepts/endures Lazzaro as a fellow prisoner. Lazzaro will arrange for and cause Billy's death in 1976 avenging Weary as promised.
Billy Pilgrim – Edgar Derby: Billy accepts Edgar Derby as a father figure.
Edgar Derby and the young men: he cares for them like a father. He is accepted by all of them. Only Lazzaro protests against him when he is elected leader of the American POWs. He would have liked that position. But he submits to the older man's authority.

Aus der Konstellation kann für die weitere Interpretation festgehalten werden, dass Billy eine absolut passive Rolle in der Handlung spielt. Diese soll später unter dem Aspekt der „Jesus-Gestalt" wieder in Erinnerung gerufen werden und wird hier noch nicht als solche thematisiert.

Die Schülerinnen und Schüler sollen klären, warum Paul Lazzaro zu Wearys „Rache-Engel" wird. Dazu sollen sie deren sehr ähnliche Charaktere vergleichen. Die Aufgabe kann als schriftliche Einzelarbeit oder als Hausaufgabe gestellt werden.

Seitenangaben werden von den Schülerinnen und Schüler nicht erwartet.

Why does Paul Lazzaro become Roland Weary's "avenging angel"?
- Compare the two characters.

They are perfect "soul-mates". Paul Lazzaro could be a twin of Roland Weary, only that he is more extreme in everything bad that was said about Roland Weary. Both have experienced bullying by the more attractive and more popular ones. Weary talks about "being ditched by others", and Lazzaro hates being "crossed" and snubbed. While Weary dreams of horrible kinds of torture, he is speaking in the abstract. Lazzaro, though, has his own ways of hurting people, made-to-measure in detail. He is the ugliest and meanest person in the whole story. The way he delights in telling perverse sadistic stories, e.g. killing a dog in a most atrocious way (p. 139), makes him disgusting to normal people. His wickedness shows not only in his eccentric liking of taking his revenge on people that "crossed" him or his friends (p. 141), but also in that it is actually the "sweetest thing" to him (p. 138). This of course makes him the perfect tool for Roland's hate and desire for vengeance. As a former "car thief" (p. 127), he has connections with criminals and will hire a professional murderer to avenge Roland one day (p. 140). He claims Roland his "buddy" died in his arms (p. 141) slightly bending the truth, because it was actually Derby who held Weary's head when he was dying. But he does this to add more weight to his oath.
As Weary, judged by his looks, seemed to be a baby-faced bear and thus rather harmless, Lazzaro in the beginning – tormented with belly aches and a broken arm, rather small and skinny – seemed harmless as well. But both are sadists and a bad kind at that. Vonnegut comments on the latter: "If he [Lazzaro] had been a dog in a city, a policeman would have shot him and sent his head to a laboratory, to see if he had rabies." (pp. 143–144)

Wenn man die bewusste Namensgebung Vonneguts mit einbezieht, ergibt sich ein weiterer Zusammenhang zwischen den beiden Figuren. Weary erliegt ermattet (= „weary") den Folgen des Wundbrandes. Lazzaro gleicht Weary in vielem: seine schwärige Haut entspricht Wearys schlimmer Wunde, ist aber auch der Spiegel seiner hässlichen Seele nach außen hin. Der biblische Lazarus war an Aussatz erkrankt und wurde durch Jesus von den Toten erweckt. Mit seiner Gestalt verbindet sich seit dem Mittelalter die Idee, dass Krankheit, Geschwüre und (Pest-)Beulen eine Strafe Gottes für begangene Sünden seien. Lazzaro scheint eine diabolische Reinkarnation Weary's in diesem Sinne zu sein.
Es ist, als habe Weary auf dem Sterbebett seinen „bösen Geist" in den willigen Gefährten eingehaucht. Dieser führt den Befehl des schrecklichen Wearys gerne aus, ist er doch genauso grausam und noch perverser veranlagt als Weary. Vonnegut hat mit ihm den äußerlich und innerlich hässlichsten Charakter der Geschichte geschaffen.
Um auf diese abstrakte Ebene der Deutung zu kommen, müssen die Namensbedeutungen geklärt werden:
„weary" = tired, worn-out;
Lazzaro = Lazarus – poor leper was risen from the dead by Jesus; people believed that such diseases were God's punishment for sinners.
Je nach Leistungsvermögen der Lerngruppe kann es sinnvoll sein, diese anspruchsvolle Interpretation als kurzen Lehrervortrag selbst zu leisten.

Nach dem Aufenthalt in dem Gefängnislager wird die Eisenbahnfahrt fortgesetzt. Die nächste Station ist das eigentliche Ziel: Dresden. Was erlebt Billy im Schlachthof Fünf und wie erlebt er die Bombardierung?

Before the inferno

Die Einfahrt nach Dresden kann mit der CD präsentiert werden (CD 4,T 3 : The temperature climbed startlingly... [10:29 min)]). Dabei sollen die Schülerinnen und Schüler den ersten Eindruck, den die Stadtsilhouette auf Billy und die Mitgefangenen macht, beschreiben. Sie sollen die anschließende Veränderung erkennen und deuten: Die zauberhaft, mystische Atmosphäre („Oz") geht über in eine surreale, groteske, die durch den clownesken Parademarsch der zerlumpten Amerikaner unter Anführung von Billy zustande kommt. Vonnegut bezeichnet die Stimmung als „light opera". Aber die heitere Leichtigkeit, das Theater ist absurd und der Männer unwürdig. Entsprechend äußert sich ein Zuschauer („surgeon") über die defätistische Darbietung, für die die POWs aber nichts können: „It was Fate, of course, which had costumed him [Billy P.] – Fate, and a feeble will to survive" (p. 151). Die Szene ist eine Militärparadentravestie, mit der Vonnegut den schönen, propagandistischen Schein von Militärparaden demontiert.

> Let's listen to Billy's first encounter with Dresden. Read along. (Text: "The temperature climbed startlingly" ... (ch. 6, p. 147) – "Fünf was good old five" (end of ch. 6, p. 153)) p. 149 155

Nach der Präsentation und dem Mitlesen beschreiben die Schülerinnen und Schüler zunächst Billys ersten Eindruck:

> What is Billy's first impression of Dresden?

Die Schülerinnen und Schüler sollen aus dem Text zitieren; die Bezeichnungen werden an der Tafel in die Spalte einer Tabelle, die später ergänzt wird, eingetragen. Dies ist die Vorbereitung.

Dresden

Billy's first encounter with the city: (p. 148)	Billy's encounter with the city after the bombing:
• the loveliest city that most of the Americans had ever seen • The skyline was intricate, voluptuous, enchanted, and absurd. • like a Sunday school picture of Heaven • Dresden had not suffered from bombings. • The radios, steam radiators, streetcars, and other things are in working order. There were theatres and restaurants. The principal enterprises (medicine, food-processing, and cigarette manufacture) are working. ➡ **"Oz"**	siehe S. 85

Von der Beschreibung ausgehend soll die eigentümliche Veränderung der Atmosphäre durch die Gefangenenparade erkannt werden:

1. Does the magical atmosphere remain throughout the prisoners' passage from the train to the slaughterhouse?

   The atmosphere remains unreal throughout the passage. But its quality changes from mystical, magical enchantment to a feeling of "light opera". This is an ironical description on the author's part. There is a change from the fascinating heavenly spell of the wizard's city of "Oz" caused by the prisoners' parade that seems odd and seemingly inappropriate for the occasion. It is surreal, too, but not in the same magical way. The mood changes into the somewhat grotesque atmosphere of a circus show. This is all due to the extraordinary clothes of the prisoners, especially of Billy, who is the leader, in a strange costume with his hands in a muff like a woman. He is dressed ridiculously and adds to the impression of a bizarre travesty parade.

2. What might the function of this scene be?

   Vonnegut wanted to show how absurd the situation is. First, soldiers march in glorious parades to show their strength and courage presenting the ideal and illusion of a glorious war and victory – then comes the reality: beaten by war, captured as prisoners by the enemy, they make a poor "fool's parade" trudging along wearily, aching and desperate, mocked at by hostile bystanders. Vonnegut ridicules this martial tradition of showing off.

Slaughterhouse-Five

Der Marsch endet im neuen Quartier, dem Schlachthofgebäude. Was ist das für eine Unterkunft, die dem Buch den Titel gab, und was erlebt Billy Pilgrim dort, bevor Dresden bombardiert wird?

Die Schülerinnen und Schüler sollen dies in Partnerarbeit schriftlich anhand ausgesuchter Textstellen bearbeiten. Die Aufgabe und die Textstellen können auf einer Folie präsentiert werden. Die Schülerinnen und Schüler können sich während oder nach dem gemeinsamen lauten Lesen die entsprechenden Passagen in ihren Texten markieren.

What was life in the slaughterhouse like for Billy Pilgrim before the bombing of Dresden?

- Work with a partner.
- Describe the building and events.
- Explore the following text passages:

	chapter/page	first and last sentence
1	ch. 6, p. 152–153	"The parade pranced ... to the gate of the Dresden slaughterhouse, and then it went inside" – "Fünf was good old five."
2	ch. 7, p. 156	"Billy thought the golliwog had something to do with World War Two, and he whispered to him his address: 'Schlachthof-fünf.'" (This was when he was found after the plane crash)
3	ch. 7, p. 157–Ch. 8, p. 165	"One of the true things was his first evening in the slaughterhouse." – "Nothing happened that night. It was the next night that about one hundred and thirty thousand people in Dresden would die."
4	ch. 8, p. 177–Ch. 8, p. 178	"He was down in the meat locker on the night that Dresden was destroyed." – "The stones were hot. Everybody else in the neighborhood was dead. So it goes."

Nach ca. 15 Minuten sollten die Schülerinnen und Schüler die wesentlichen Punkte stichwortartig erfasst haben. Für die gemeinsame Ergebnissicherung kann man bereits vor Beginn der Partnerarbeit einem oder mehreren Paaren Folien zum sofortigen Übertragen ihrer Ergebnisse geben. Man kann dann gleich nach der Arbeitsphase entweder mit den Ergebnissen des einen Paares arbeiten, oder bei mehreren Vorlagen diese am OHP besprechen und zusammenfügen:

What was life in the slaughterhouse like for Billy Pilgrim before the bombing of Dresden?

1. The slaughterhouse:

- was not a busy place any more.
- was where the Americans were taken to the fifth building inside the gate, with a big number five over the door.
- was a one-story cement block cube with sliding doors in the front and the back.
- had been a shelter for pigs about to be butchered.
- was now home for one hundred American prisoners of war.
- had bunks inside, two potbellied stoves, and a water tap with a latrine behind it.

2. The significance:

- Their English-speaking guard told them to memorize their address in case they got lost in the big city of "Schlachthof-fünf".
- The address is engraved in Billy's memory: he repeats it automatically over and over again after the plane crash.

3. Events taking place during the prisoners' time of residence:

- On their way to the communal kitchen, they are led the wrong way by the sixteen-year old German Werner Gluck. They open the dressing room of female German refugees. The teenage girls in there were naked and were scared to death by the sight of the men. Billy and Werner Gluck had never seen a naked woman before.
- Billy and the others work at a malt syrup factory as cleaners and secretly "spoon" some of the syrup that is made for pregnant women. Spooning was a crime, but everybody did it. Billy feeds Derby with a "syrup-lollipop" through the window like a baby. Derby bursts out in tears of thankfulness.
- Howard W. Campbell, Jr., the American who had become a Nazi, visits the slaughterhouse and spreads his propaganda in favour of Hitler. He wants to recruit men for a German military unit called "The Free American Corps".
- Derby rises to the occasion and "has his moment in his life". He offends Campbell by calling him "something much lower than a snake or a rat – or even a blood-filled tick" and delivers a moving speech on American values like democracy, freedom, equal opportunity, fairness, and other values, arguing fervently against the "disease of Nazism". He is interrupted by air-raid sirens.

4. The air raid and destruction of Dresden

- Everybody rushes to shelter in a meat locker under the slaughterhouse. The meat locker had empty hooks for thousands of animals. Nothing happens that night. It was the next night…

The destruction of Dresden

Die Schülerinnen und Schüler sollen in Einzelarbeit schriftlich erörtern, warum Vonnegut das Schlachthaus zum Haupttitel seines Romans gemacht hat. Dabei sollen sie die erarbeiteten Ereignisse diskutieren und die entscheidende Textstelle mit einbeziehen: ch. 8, p. 177 – p. 178 („He was down in the meat locker on the night that Dresden was destroyed" – „Tell me a story,"…). Die Aufgabenstellung und Textstelle werden laut gelesen, dann beginnt die Stillarbeit, oder die Aufgabe geht in die häusliche Vorbereitung.

Explain why Vonnegut called the novel *Slaughterhouse-Five* in the first place. Consider Billy's experiences that we just have dealt with in this context and additionally the night of the bombing. (ch. 8, p. 177–p. 178: "He was down in the meat locker on the night that Dresden was destroyed."– "Tell me a story …")

The most obvious reason for the first title of the novel is that Billy Pilgrim experienced the bombing in Dresden in the slaughterhouse. He survived there in the underground meat locker.
There were cadavers hanging around, and the symbolism is striking. Billy has witnessed manslaughter on the battlefield and its continuation then upstairs in the city of Dresden.
But the butchered animals had one privilege. They were somehow killed in dignity – first anesthetized and then killed for a purpose: to feed humans. Soldiers did not receive such graces. They were killed fully aware of the atrocity and the purpose is extremely suspect.
In a conversation with a Tralfamadorian on their ability to live in eternal peace, Billy gives a short account of human affairs and draws a succinct image of a species engaged in permanent war, pointing out the fact that humans slaughter humans. ("I am from a planet that has been engaged in senseless slaughter since the beginning of time", p. 116)
The night in the meat locker has more to it than just being a place of survival for Billy. It is also a place of traumatizing fear. The room is described as cool and dark. The men are as if in a trap. Only one of the guards ventures a few glimpses out of the door to watch what is going on. He gives a classical "viewing from the walls" – here door – to the others as in the old dramas. The others depend on this report. It is a claustrophobic situation that will engrave itself into Billy's memory. He feels like the empty hooks around him were waiting for him and the others to be hung up there. The room is very safe, but what will await them when they get out? Will they be shot right at the door? What will the city look like? The situation is scary, uncanny, and unreal.
When he finally sees the "moonscape" of that once splendid city he cannot believe it. He did not see the act of destruction – he is faced with the plain fact that the city has disappeared. How could he comprehend such an instant transformation?

Billy erzählt diesen einschneidenden Moment seines Lebens Montana auf Tralfamodore. Hier erzählt er auch, wie es nach der Bombardierung aussah und weiterging. Die Schilderung und das Ende des achten Kapitels kann mit der CD gelesen werden. Die Hör-/Leseaufgabe zum Unterstreichen lautet:

Mark all the passages that tell about how Dresden changed after the air raid.

CD 5/T 1 "Tell me a story," Montana Wildhack said … (5:43)
Text: ch. 8, pp. 178 – 181.

Die Ergebnisse werden besprochen und dann in der vormals angelegten Tabelle zu Dresden eingetragen (s. S. 80, 85)

Dresden

Billy's first encounter with the city (p. 148):

- It was the loveliest city that most of the Americans had ever seen.
- The skyline was intricate, voluptuous, enchanted, and absurd.
- It was like a Sunday school picture of Heaven.
- Dresden had not suffered from bombings.
- Radios, steam radiators, streetcars and other things are in working order. There were theatres and restaurants. The principal enterprises (medicine, food-processing, and cigarette manufacture) are working.

➡ Oz

Billy's encounter with the city after the bombing (pp. 177–181):

- Dresden was one big flame.
- The sky was black with smoke.
- There was a firestorm.
- The sun was an angry little pinhead.
- The stones were hot
- Everybody else in the neighborhood was dead.
- Fenceposts, windows and roofs of stockyards were gone.
- There were "little logs" lying around – charred corpses
- The buildings had collapsed, their wood had been consumed, and their stones had crashed down.

➡ the moon

Der Vergleich, „Dresden vor und nach der Bombardierung", kann in einem Interview mit Billy als Überlebendem der Brandkatastrophe eingebracht werden. Ein Zeitungs- oder Radioteam begegnet den durch die Ruinen wandelnden Gefangenen und interviewt die Überlebenden. Billy soll so befragt werden, dass er seinen ersten Eindruck von der Stadt und seine Gefühle nach der Zerstörung wiedergibt. Das Interview mit Billy kann im Unterricht in Partnerarbeit oder Kleingruppenarbeit vorbereitet und als Hausaufgabe ausgearbeitet werden:

> Imagine that a newspaper or radio-team has made it through to Dresden to interview the survivors of the catastrophe. They meet Billy Pilgrim and want to know about his impressions and feelings after the destruction of the city.
> Write down the interview and act it out with your partner.

On the way to Dresden – group task

- Give an account on what Billy Pilgrim experiences on the way to Dresden. Work in groups on the passages from the text provided:

Group 1: The prisoners' march

Text:
ch. 3, p. 55 "So Weary and Billy were both without decent military footwear now, and they had to walk for miles and miles ..." – p. 65 "There were rows and rows of boxcars waiting."

Group 2: What happens on the boxcar ride?

Text:
ch. 3, p. 65 "There were rows and rows of boxcars waiting" – p. 70 "Now the train began to creep eastward."

Group 3: What was it like to be in the boxcar for the prisoners and their guards? and Part 1 – what happens in the prison camp?

Text:
ch. 4, p. 77 "When he regained consciousness ... He was in a boxcar crossing Germany again." – ch. 5 p. 85 "Billy gurgled and cooed."

Group 4: Part 2 – what happens in the prison camp?

Text:
Ch. 5, p. 90 "Billy went from total dark to total light, found himself back in the war, in the delousing station again." – p. 99 "Now he read it again while Billy Pilgrim entered a morphine paradise."
p. 105 "He opened one eye, saw poor old Edgar Derby ..." – p. 107 "So the Americans put their weapons down ... if they possibly could."
p. 123 "He groped for light ... he had traveled back to 1944, to the prison hospital again" – p. 126 "So Billy buttoned his pants."

Group 5: Why is Howard Campbell cited in the prison camp and what is going on there?

Text:
ch. 5, p. 127 "At three in the morning on Billy's morphine night in prison ..." – p. 131 They despised any leader ... that he should stop putting on airs."; ch. 6, p. 136 – p. 141 "Whenever the doorbell rings, have somebody else answer the door." – p. 145 "Then he swings back into life again ..." – p. 147 "And so on."

Component 6

Tralfamadore

Wieso ausgerechnet Billy? Die Schülerinnen und Schüler sollen zunächst die Umstände der Entführung und die Beschreibung der Außerirdischen und ihres Planeten erfassen und kreativ umsetzen. In einer zweiten Sequenz geht es darum, Billys Zustand der Transzendenz aufgrund der Tralfamadorianischen Philosophie zu verstehen und dann in einem weiteren Schritt Vonneguts Ansinnen damit zu erkennen und zu formulieren. Als Einstieg bietet sich klassisch an, einen Tralfamadorianer malen zu lassen gemäß der Beschreibung (ch. 2, p. 26):

- What does a Tralfamadorian look like? Draw one!

Die „Kunst"-Aktion sollte wirklich spontan stattfinden, sonst könnte es sein, dass die Schülerinnen und Schüler ein Internet-Fertigprodukt mitbringen. Dort gibt es massenweise Bilder. Mit dem Gemälde kann zur Talkshow-Aktivität übergegangen werden.

6.1 The science fiction factor

Billy Pilgrim, a hostage in Tralfamadore

Die für mindestens eine Doppelstunde angelegte, hochkommunikative Übungsform der Talkshow kann mit folgender Ankündigung eingeleitet werden:

- Billy has told people that he had been kidnapped by the Tralfamadorians in a flying saucer. Now the media is hot for the story in detail. They invite Billy and Barbara to the famous talk show "TalkingHeads". There will also be scientists and a psychologist. You will be watched by the television audience.

Für die Bestimmung der Rollen können die vorgefertigten *role cards* ***(Copy 14, S. 96)*** benutzt werden. Die *audience*-Karten werden nach „Restgruppenstärke" kopiert. Dabei sollte beachtet werden, dass es zwei Sorten gibt: Die „couch potato"- und die „critical middle-class info watcher"-Variante. Die Karten sind so konzipiert, dass die Schülerinnen und Schüler ihre Rolle mimisch und gestisch gestalten können. Es gibt Tipps für das Verhalten und die Erwartungen der Personen. Um eine schöne und gehaltvolle Spielaktion zu erzielen, sollte den Schülerinnen und Schülern genügend Zeit zur Vorbereitung der Rolle gegeben werden. Gerne kann die Sache zu einer Parodie werden (*mock talk*), aber bei aller möglichen Albernheit soll inhaltlich viel umgesetzt werden. Der oder die Moderierende (Mr or Ms Smart) der wöchentlichen Talkshow „TalkingHeads" sollte Sorge dafür tragen, dass die Redeanteile möglichst ausgewogen sind.
Wenn die Darbietung richtig gut gelingt, vielleicht als *mock talk*, warum es nicht wagen und gegebenenfalls einmal den Parallelkurs, der womöglich auch gerade die Lektüre bearbeitet, zur Show einladen? Diese hochkommunikative Übung setzt den gesamten Inhalt über die Entführung mit der fliegenden Untertasse und den „Zoo-Aufenthalt" mit Montana Wild-

hack auf Tralfamadore um. Vieles der vorangegangenen Stunden wird wiederholt. Es wird intensiv gesprochen und hoffentlich auch gelacht!

Die philosophischen Lehren der Tralfamadorianer sind so wichtig für die Gesamtbedeutung des Werkes, dass deren Deutung eine intensivere Erarbeitung im Anschluss an den „Science fiction"-Aspekt der Handlung gewidmet wird.
Schriftlich wird die Talkshow wiederum in einer gestaltenden Aufgabe gesichert:

- For your homework: imagine you have watched the show. Tell your friends on social networks (*Schülerverzeichnis*, *Facebook* or the like) about it. Be emotional!

Oder man wählt für diese Art der Rezension die „altmodische" Form des Telefonats mit einem Freund oder einer Freundin.

Is *Slaughterhouse-Five* a science fiction novel?

Die Frage wird in der Literaturwissenschaft in der Tat kontrovers diskutiert. Einerseits liegen spezifische Kennzeichen des *science fiction*-Genres vor: Die Außerirdischen mit ihrem „ Pömpelkörper" und dem gelben Glotzauge im Handteller (p. 76), die fliegende Untertasse, die klassische Entführung eines „Erdlings" durch einen Saugstrahl, der Planet mit seiner für Menschen giftigen Atmosphäre und natürlich Billys Sprünge in der Zeit.
Andererseits deutet vieles darauf hin, dass Tralfamadore nur das Fantasiekonstrukt eines hirngeschädigten Kriegsveteranen mit post-traumatischen Wahnvorstellungen ist. Die Schülerinnen und Schüler sollen sich dennoch auf den *science fiction*-Faktor einlassen und dann diskutieren, inwieweit sie den Roman als *science fiction*-Literatur einstufen würden. Dabei werden besonders die Rolle Billys als Missionar der außerirdischen Philosophie sowie ebendiese zu entscheidenden Kriterien. Die Stoffsammlung kann insbesondere aus chapter 5, p. 100ff. erfolgen.
Wenn die Sequenz mit der Schülerrezension der Talkshow begonnen hat, so kann das Thema „*science fiction*" daran anknüpfen. Hat man aus Zeitgründen die groß angelegte Talkshow auslassen müssen, so gibt z. B. das Bild des Tralfamadorianers den nötigen Impuls:

- Is *Slaughterhouse-Five* a science fiction novel?

Das Thema bietet sich für eine klassische Pro-und Contra-Diskussion an. Um die Schülerinnen und Schüler aber nicht mit Aktivitäten zu überfordern, wird man diese je nachdem ausführen: wenn nicht gerade die große Talkshow stattgefunden hat, bietet sich hier eine kreative Umsetzung, z. B. als Zweiparteiendebatte an.
Wenn aber schon gespielt wurde, dann empfiehlt sich eher eine ruhigere schriftliche Erarbeitung zu zweit oder auch einzeln nach einem sondierenden Unterrichtsgespräch. Dabei können entweder gleich Notizen für die Stoffsammlung an der Tafel gemacht werden, oder aus den vorgelesenen Arbeiten werden z. B. folgende Aspekte zum Thema gesichert:

Is *Slaughterhouse-Five* a science fiction novel?

Pro

- Billy's jumping in time, the time travelling
- Billy ascertains that his ability to travel in time has nothing to do with the Tralfamadorians.
- the kidnapping by the flying saucer from Tralfamadore
- Tralfamadore – an extraterrestrial place and planet with a different atmosphere
- Vonnegut has written science fiction short stories and novels and is renowned for that kind of literature.
- The novel *Slaughterhouse-Five* is classified as a science fiction novel in some acknowledged literary classifications.
- Science fiction literature was very *en vogue* in the late 60s because of the governmental space programme. The hippies believed in life in outer space and the "age of Aquarius", etc. So it served as a bible for these seekers of esoteric meaning.

Contra

- Billy tells the story in 1968. At that time he already suffers from brain damage caused in the plane crash and also from PTSD.
- The idea of Tralfamadore comes from a novel written by Kilgore Trout. Billy got to know his literature by sharing a hospital room with the writer's greatest fan, Mr Rosewater.
- In a typical science fiction novel, there is more action and less philosophical talk.
- The part with the Tralfamadorians is on the surface an element of science fiction but it does not determine the whole character of the novel.
- Vonnegut made good use of the science fiction element because
  a) science fiction was *en vogue*
  b) it is an established means of expressing social criticism (cf. utopias)
  c) one can speak one's mind freely in the harmless conditional form or the disguise of alien characters, but the novel's character is that of an anti-war book as the author points out in his preface-like frame in Chapters 1 and 10.

Conclusion

The novel has an important science fictional element but it is an anti-war novel in the first place. The determination of the "right" genre would not have troubled Vonnegut since he was a dedicated writer of science fiction and prophetic epics. In the novel, he states the function of science fiction for the rebuilding of Dresden ironically:
"So, they [the Dresdeners] were trying to re-invent themselves and their universe. Science fiction was a big help." (p. 101)

Das Zitat über die Funktion von *science fiction* für den Wiederaufbau Dresdens kann in Hinblick auf die positive Chance einer friedlichen Utopie abschließend diskutiert werden oder als Essay-Aufgabe häuslich bearbeitet werden.

6.2 Billy Pilgrim as a prophet of the Tralfamadorian philosophy

Billy, der angeblich nur eine Mikrosekunde lang von der Erde verschwunden war und in dieser Zeit sein Abenteuer auf Tralfamadore erlebt hat (p. 26), ist nach seiner Rückkehr beseelt von der Idee, den Menschen die außerirdische Philosophie mitzuteilen. Am Ende des Romans wird er nach einem Auftritt im Radio höflich aber bestimmt aus dem Studio geworfen (p. 206), am Anfang des Romans sehen wir ihn an der Schreibmaschine sitzend, Briefe über die Tralfamadorianer verfassend (p. 28 ff.). Er fühlt sich zum Prophet berufen und sieht sogar seinen Beruf im Dienste dieser Aufklärung. Besonders was Billy Pilgrim über die Ansicht, was Zeit bedeutet, gelernt hat und damit über die Bedeutung von Leben und Tod, steht im Mittelpunkt. Die Stunde könnte einen musikalischen Auftakt und ein musikalisches Ende bekommen.

Die Motivation für die „Philosophie"-Stunde kann mit dem Song der *Scorpions* „Still loving you" angeregt werden.[1] ***(Copy 15, Song 1, S. 98)***. Es handelt sich zwar um ein Liebeslied, aber der Sänger trifft genau eines der Probleme, die auch Billy Pilgrim anspricht: Wenn man die Zeit zurückdrehen könnte, dann könnte man Fehler ungeschehen machen oder ganz vermeiden. Im Lied möchte der Sänger die Geliebte zurückgewinnen, Billy Pilgrim erlebt kurz vor seiner Entführung das „Rückwärtslaufen" eines Filmes über den Krieg und ist fasziniert von der Idee, was wäre, wenn es möglich wäre, auf diese Art und Weise schlimme Dinge rückgängig machen zu können (ch. 4, pp. 74 – 75).

In dieser Sequenz soll Billy's Lehre von den Tralfamadorians für die Menschheit herausgestellt werden. Es läuft auf das Motto des Buches hinaus „So it goes – life goes on – that's the way it is!". Es geht um die aufmunternde Aufforderung der Tralfamadorianer an die Menschen, nur die "happy moments in life" anzusehen und alle schlechten zu ignorieren. Darin steckt ein Gutteil Fatalismus. Aber es ist ein positives Akzeptieren des Schicksals gemäß der Parole: "Let the good times roll!" Mit dem gleichnamigen Song der *Cars* kann die Stunde beispielsweise abgerundet werden ***(Copy 15, Song 2, S. 98)***. Die Überleitung zu der Funktion als Antikriegsroman in der Zeit der 60er-Jahre lässt sich so leicht herstellen.

Der Ablauf der Sequenz sieht folgende Unterrichtsschritte vor:

1. Einstimmung auf das Thema durch den Song „Still loving you" von den *Scorpions*. Die Schülerinnen und Schüler sollen einen Bezug herstellen:

   - What does this song have to do with Billy Pilgrim's experiences with the Tralfamadorians?

- Die Schülerinnen und Schüler erkennen die Zeitthematik.
- Das Stichwort "clown" kann zweifach gedeutet werden, zum einen ist Billy in dem Zoo ein Clown für die Tralfamadorianer, er wird aber ja auch im Roman immer wieder als Clown bezeichnet.
- Er lernt von den Tralfamadorians, dass das egal sein kann. Auch diese Zeit ist nur ein Moment, den er ja ausblenden kann, wenn er sich auf die guten Zeiten konzentriert.

---

[1] Wenn man das Lied nicht greifbar hat, kann es legal über Online-Anbieter heruntergeladen werden, oder vielleicht bringen Schülerinnen und Schüler die beiden vorgeschlagenen Songs mit. Dann ist allerdings der als Motivation gedachte Überraschungseffekt weg. Bitte lassen Sie sich nur eindeutige Kaufversionen geben, und beachten Sie die für Ihr Bundesland geltenden Regeln zum Datenschutz, Urheber- und Aufführungsrecht in Hinblick auf Ihren Status als öffentliche oder halböffentliche Person. Dies gilt insbesondere auch für die empfohlene Einspielung der Filmsequenz oder des ganzen Filmes.

2. Das Thema des „Rückgängigmachens" wurde oben erklärt, hier findet sich eine starke Parallele und ein direkter Bezug zu der Entführungsnacht, in der Billy den Film ansieht, um die Wartezeit auf das UFO zu überbrücken. Das Ereignis kann gemeinsam nachgelesen werden:
   ch. 4, pp. 74–75: "It was a movie about American bombers in the Second World War ...– and then it was time to go out into his backyard to meet the flying saucer."
   Wenn absehbar ist, dass man eventuell am Ende der Einheit nicht dazu kommt, den Film zu zeigen, dann sollte man vielleicht auf einen oder beide Songs verzichten und lieber die Szene zeigen! Der Einsatz aller Medien wäre wohl eine Überfrachtung der Stunde. Die Filmszene kann generell eine Option sein. Bitte beachten Sie die geltenden Datenschutzbestimmungen.

3. Hierauf folgt die zentrale Frage:

   - What does Billy learn from the Tralfamadorians?

Um den Inhalt der Tralfamadorianischen Philosophie erfassen zu können, können anhand der *Reading Companions* und des Textes relevante Textstellen in Partnerarbeit gesucht werden. Oder die betreffenden Textstellen werden den Schülerinnen und Schülern zum Auswerten und Markieren genannt. Einige Passagen können wahlweise vor der Bearbeitung erst laut miteinander gelesen und vorab auf ihren Informationswert bezüglich der Frage beurteilt werden. Die Aufgabenstellung und die Seitenangaben können auf Folie projiziert werden, damit die Schülerinnen und Schüler auch während der Erarbeitungsphase orientiert bleiben:

What does Billy learn from the Tralfamadorians and what does he learn about them?

Explore the following text passages for information:

1. ch. 2, pp. 26–27 ..."which is 'So it goes'". (p. 27)
2. ch. 4, pp. 76–77 The kidnapping
3. ch. 4, pp. 85–86 "He was strapped to a yellow contour chair ... any talk of free will."
4. ch. 5, pp. 86–87 Tralfamadorian reading
5. ch. 5 pp. 112, 113–117 "Escape was out of the question ... miles away"; "Now the first question came ...'Um,' said Billy Pilgrim"
6. ch. 7, p. 154 (one paragraph only) "Lionel Merbel was a machine ... and waving bye-bye."
7. ch. 9, pp. 194–195 (one paragraph only) "Billy stayed in the wagon [...] His sun-drenched snooze in the back of the wagon."
8. ch.10, pp. 210–211 "On Tralfamadore, says Billy Pilgrim, there isn't much interest in Jesus ... I'm grateful that so many moments are nice."

Je nach Leistungsfähigkeit der Lerngruppe kann es nun den Schülerinnen und Schülern selbst überlassen werden, die Aufgabe sinnvoll zu strukturieren, oder man hilft, indem man ein paar Leitfragen anschließt, zur Binnenstrukturierung vorgibt oder nach dem Ansehen und ggf. Lesen der Textstellen diese gemeinsam an der Tafel entwickelt:

What does Billy Pilgrim learn from the Tralfamadorians and what does he learn about them?

Checklist for the passages:

- What are the Tralfamadorians like? (e.g. outer appearance, behaviour towards Billy and Montana, etc.)
- What do they think about humans and what do they know about them?
- What is their attitude towards war and murder and the end of the universe?
- What is their attitude towards time, life, and death?
- What are they especially interested in and would like to teach the Earthlings?

Für eine schnellere Vorgehensweise können die oben aufgeführten Textstellen mit den Leitfragen auch zusammenkopiert werden und an die Schülerinnen und Schüler verteilt werden. Die Leitfragen können dann auf Kleingruppen verteilt werden. Die Arbeitsteilung erspart viel Zeit. Ca. 20 Minuten dürften den Gruppen reichen, um ihren jeweiligen Bereich am Text zu belegen. Die Ergebnisse sollen auf Folien übertragen präsentiert werden. Hier wird zum Auffinden der Textstellen ausführlicher zitiert, im Unterricht genügen sinnvolle Stichworte:

What are the Tralfamadorians like?

- Their outer appearance is that of a green, plumber's suction cup with a small hand on top and an eye in the palm (p. 26).
- They can see in four dimensions and pity the Earthlings for not having that ability (p. 26)
- They have five sexes instead of two.
- They are curious researchers and keen readers.
- Their planet has a toxic atmosphere of cyanide and is 446.120.000.000.000.000 miles away from the Earth (p. 112).
- They treat Billy and Montana friendly like pets or animals at a zoo. For their comfort the Tralfamadorians do their best (p. 112f.f).
- They do not understand the human perception of time and they think it is gibberish (p. 114).

What do they think and know about humans?

- People's behaviour at funerals is strange to them. They think human beings are silly (p. 27).
- Chronology is just an illusion of Earthlings: they think that one moment follows the other like beads on a string and that once a moment is gone it is gone forever (p. 27).
- They see humans "as great millipedes – with babies' legs at one end and old peoples' legs at the other," (p. 87).
- They found out that there are seven sexes among the humans for reproduction (p. 114).
- They try to explain the "human condition" by using a "metaphor" because they could not imagine what time looked like. They imagine that an "Earthling" was encased in a metal sphere which he could never take off. With this he was strapped on a flatcar that moved him, but had no choice of the direction he was going or to what event (pp. 114–115).
- They are the only specimen of life in the whole universe having a concept of "free will", so it is nothing really that matters too much, just a human eccentricity signifying nothing (p. 86).
- So they conclude that human beings are machines, which they do not necessarily find negative (p. 154).

What is their attitude towards war and murder and the end of the universe?

- They have wars but they simply ignore them. They don't like them (p. 117).
- Wars on earth cannot be prevented; they will always happen. So anti-war activities are nonsense (p. 117).
- The universe looks like a heaven "filled with rarefied luminous spaghetti" to them (p. 87).
- It will never be man's fault to blow it; they have blown it already, and will do it again; it is just a momentary mistake by a Tralfamadorian pilot experimenting with new fuels for the flying saucers. He presses the wrong button and off the Universe blows! It needn't be prevented because it is just a moment structured that way (p. 117).

What is their attitude towards time, life and death?

- They have the ability to see in four dimensions; they can see time (p. 26).
- For them, "all moments, past , present and future, always have existed, always will exist; they can see how permanent all the moments are, and they can look at any moment that interests them" (p. 27).
- Chronology is just an illusion of Earthlings: they think that one moment follows the other like beads on a string and that once a moment is gone it is gone forever (p. 27).
- When a person dies, he only appears to die. He is still very much alive in the past, so death is not final (pp. 26–27).
- For them, time has permanence and everything is simultaneous: "All time is all time" (p. 86).
- Time in the earthly sense is incomprehensible for them as their conception is to Billy. They need to explain it with metaphors: Billy's question on why he had been picked among all living creatures is answered with the explanation that it was due to the moment; it was the moment that happened to him like the amber that encases the insect happened to flow over it at the decisive moment in the insects life (p. 77).

What are they especially interested in and would like to teach the Earthlings?

- They are interested in studying human beings in a scientific way.
- They are interested in novels written in the Tralfamadorian style, that is in telegrams because they love reading symbols and messages and rejoice in the "depth of marvelous moments" (p. 88).
- They are only interested in good moments and ignore bad ones:
  "That's one thing Earthlings might learn to do, if they tried hard enough: ignore the awful times, and concentrate on the good ones" (p. 117).
- They are not much interested in Jesus Christ but in Charles Darwin instead (p. 210).

Nach der Vorstellung und Besprechung der Ergebnisse gilt es, das eigentliche Fazit zu ziehen:

- What is the Tralfamadorian lore after all?

Die Antworten werden an der Tafel unter der Überschrift „The Tralfamadorian Mantra" festgehalten und notiert:

The Tralfamadorian Mantra

Fragen Sie die Schülerinnen und Schüler nach einer noch unkomplizierteren Übersetzung der Lebensweisheit.

- How would you express their "motto" for mankind in your own words?

Die Tralfamadorians scheinen recht hedonistisch veranlagt zu sein in ihrem fatalistischen Gleichmut, sodass auch Sprüche wie „Live life deeply", „Think positive", oder das berühmte „Always look on the bright side of life" von Monty Python sich aufdrängen. Letzteres ließe sich auch zum Ausklang musikalisch einbringen.[1] Die Variante „Let the good times roll" passt thematisch in jeder Hinsicht sehr gut. Zum Abschluss könnte der Song der *Cars* gespielt werden ***(Copy 15, Song 2, S. 98)***. Der Text bietet eine gute Überleitung zum nächsten

[1] Der Film, aus dem das Lied stammt, *The Life of Brian*, ist in der Tat „artverwandt". Schwarzer Humor, Zweifel an Gott und der Bestimmung des menschlichen Lebens und die letzte Erkenntnis, dass alles so geschieht, wie es geschieht, prägen diese parodistische „Jesusverwechslungsgeschichte." Eventuell eine mögliche *post reading activity*, wenn man auf Vonneguts Umgang mit der Religion intensiver eingeht.

und letzten inhaltlichen Gegenstand: des Anti-Kriegsromans und die Zeit der 60er-Jahre, in der er entstanden ist.

Die Hausaufgabe soll erklären, warum Billy zum „Guru" der Tralfamadorianer wird und was er von ihnen verkünden will:

- What is Billy's calling? Comment on the reasons why Billy thinks that he has a mission to spread the Tralfamadorian philosophy among the Earthlings.

Für die Erörterung wird von der Textstelle ch. 2, p. 29 ausgegangen:

> "And Billy, meanwhile, was trying to hang onto his dignity, to persuade Barbara and everybody else that he was far from senile, that on the contrary, he was devoting himself to a calling much higher than mere business. Billy believed, because they could not see as well as his little green friends on Tralfamadore."

Lösungsvorschlag:
Billy feels like "the chosen one" because the Tralfamadorians seem to be Gods. They can see in four dimensions and simultaneously look at time all at once. Death and the future mean nothing to them; they need not fear anything. Their mental state seems to be that of "transcendence, that is, they are on a "higher stage" of consciousness judging human affairs with detachment and pity. Billy has come to know them as caring and protecting creatures, much better than a God who lets dehumanization happen according to the laws of the "survival of the fittest". The Tralfamadorian idea of death is consolation. It is inevitable and, at the same time, irrelevant. They wish, however, they could keep the moment to save people from death. Billy is enlightened in that way that by following the Tralfamadorian principle of equanimity and only looking at the happy moments of life, he can bring about real peace for mankind. As a matter of fact, Billy, the former assistant to a chaplain in war turns away from Christian religion. He is said to never have gone to church any more after his Tralfamadorian conversion (cf. p. 85).

Mit der Musik endet die Stunde (s.o.) und die Einheit zu den Tralfamadorianern. Die erteilte Hausaufgabe weist auf den letzten Themenblock, die Deutung und Bedeutung des Buches als Anti-Kriegsroman, hin. Die Tralfamadorianer sind offensichtlich Vonneguts Mahner wider die menschliche Torheit , und es war zu sehen, dass er sich ihre literarische Art von „brief, urgent messages" in der Form von „clumps of symbols" (p. 88) angeeignet hat für seine „urgent message": Nie wieder Krieg!

Role cards for the talk show "TalkingHeads"

You are: Billy Pilgrim

- Say "hello" to the people. ☺
- Be authentic. Be obstinate.
- Watch out for Barbara who tries to calm you down and declares you senile. She is having a good time in the limelight (*Rampenlicht*) …
- Stick to your point: Tralfamadore does exist – give an emotional description when asked about it.
- Do indulge in (*schwelgen*) the memories of Montana but keep your language decent.
- Be glad about the great mental enlightenment (*Aufklärung/Erhellung*) you have received from the Tralfamadorians but keep your feet on the ground for now because …
- … you are not mad; the kidnapping was real and not a consequence of the brain damage caused in the plane crash.

You are: Barbara, Billy's daughter

- Oh, how embarrassing this is but see it positively:
- Say "hello" to the people. ☺
- Weird, old Daddy has brought you into the limelight (*Rampenlicht*).
- Let Daddy talk for a while but always be attentive and ready to fall in and interrupt him when you feel embarrassed.
- You can explain to the audience why Billy has this "fixed idea" of having been kidnapped:
  – those Trout books
  – such horrible shocks: first the war and then his mother's death.
- Don't be shy. Look at you – you are a kind of star right now!
- You could steal the show from Daddy and have a really good time … ;-)
- By the way, the psychologist takes sides with you.

You are: the presenter, Mr/Ms Smart

- What a strange show this is tonight.
- Introduce your guests and let them say: "Hello!" (They have been trained to do this … ☺)
- Tell the audience about the subject of the show.
- Have Billy talk first and see what will follow.
- Keep an eye on Barbara – she might steal the show from Daddy…
- Intervene in case of disagreements that might escalate into arguments.
- If the participants are at a loss as to what to say, give them the necessary clues.
- You need to know everything on the kidnapping, the flying saucer's interior, and the Tralfamadorians, including their looks, habits, etc.
- Finish the show with a brief statement on the evening and say something like: "Thank you and good-bye until next week: same place, same chronologically fixed ti me!"

You are: A scientific UFO-researcher

- The time of your life! Say "hello" to the people ☺
- Here is the living proof for your theory.
- There is life out there!
- Ask about the kidnapping, how could Billy "sense" that he would be fetched?
- Talk about other people with similar experiences.
- Talk about the possibilities of making contact with these aliens.
- Support Billy in everything!
- Watch out for the unbelieving colleague next to you – cut him or her short. ☺

You are: a serious scientist

- Oh, no, not again!
- Another lunatic yelling (*herumposaunen*) about flying saucers and the existence of extra-terrestrial life – what a drag! But:
- Say "hello". ☺
- You are a convinced "unbeliever".
- All your data, statistics, diagrams, and computations prove there is no life out there – basta.
- Cut that UFO idiot short but don't neglect your scientific high-brow manners and discipline. You know it's not worth it; this is just too low standard anyway… ☺

You are: a psychologist

- What a typical, classical case of PTSD! You are delighted with having such a typical example in front of you but you also pity Billy and, even more, the one who is suffering most from such a family tragedy, Barbara.
- Say "hello" ☺.
- Take sides with Barbara.
- Give a detached (objective) evaluation of how you see the case in clinical terms.
- Support your statements with examples from your clinical practice.
- Offer help to Billy and Barbara and give them your address and contact details to book weekly sessions with you.
- Yes, you may rejoice: that case will make your cashier (Kassenautomat) run hot … ☺

You are: a member of the audience (style: "couch potato" ☺)

- Come on, it's not too bad –
- O.K. there will probably be no crisps or other snacks that you usually munch on while watching the telly, but today is different anyway. You wouldn't even find your mouth because you're so excited:
- A real hostage from an alien planet – live! Great! Sensational!
- Does he convince you?
- Can the scientists convince you?
- Are the three scientists influencing him regarding his "fixed idea"?
- How do you feel about Barbara?
- Does the presenter do a good job?
- What would you have asked the participants if you had been there?
- Remember: you have missed your usual soap for this show that you generally find "pathetic" (*scheußlich*) because of the political humbug …
- Watch the people and take notes on statements, behaviour or whatever "upsets" you.
- Give feedback on the performance in the authentic style of your role.

You are: a member of the audience (style: critical middle-class observer of the current scene)

- Your favourite programme is on and what a superb topic again!
- However, keep a sceptical mind.
- Does that self-acclaimed alien hostage convince you?
- Can the scientists convince you?
- Are the three scientists influencing him regarding his "fixed idea"?
- How do you feel about Barbara?
- Does the presenter do a good job?
- What would you have asked the participants if this had been your role?
- Remember: you are used to quality in this show and expect it too.
- Watch the people, take notes on statements, behaviour or whatever "upsets" you.
- Give feedback on the performance in the authentic style of your role.

Live life the Tralfamadorian way: let the good times roll!

The Scorpions: Still loving you

Time, it needs time
To win back your love again
I will be there, I will be there
Love, only love
Can bring back your love someday
I will be there, I will be there

I'll fight, babe, I'll fight
To win back your love again
I will be there, I will be there
Love, only love
Can break down the wall someday
I will be there, I will be there

If we'd go again
All the way from the start
I would try to change
The things that killed our love
Your pride has built a wall, so strong
That I can't get through
Is there really no chance
To start once again
I'm loving you

Try, baby try
To trust in my love again
I will be there, I will be there
Love, our love
Just shouldn't be thrown away
I will be there, I will be there

The Cars: Good times roll

Let the good times roll
Let them knock you around
Let the good times roll
Let them make you a clown

Let them leave you up in the air
Let them brush your rock and roll hair

Let the good times roll
Let the good times roll
Let the good times roll

Let the stories be told
They can say what they want
Let the photos be old
Let them show what they want

Let them leave you up in the air
Let them brush your rock and roll hair
Let the good times roll
Let the good times roll
Won't you let the good times roll?

Good times roll

If the illusion is real
Let them give you a ride
If they got thunder appeal
Let them be on your side

Let them leave you up in the air
Let them brush your rock and roll hair
Let the good times roll
Won't you let the good times roll
Let the good times roll

because…

Component 7

The anti-war novel

7.1 The style: Tralfamadorian style and black humour

Wir erinnern uns an das Vorwort, in dem Vonnegut sein Verpflichtetsein gegenüber den Tralfamadorianern kundtut, denn er habe ihre „telegrapic" und daher „schizophrenic" Art der Literatur übernommen. Nur so war es ihm möglich, „massacre", das Kriegsmassaker zu beschreiben, das er erlebt hat.

Dieser „Tralfamadorianische Stil" hat den Roman tatsächlich bestimmt: die flickenhafte Struktur entspricht den „telegrams" und „clumps of symbols", wobei Vonnegut die Vorliebe der Tralfamadorianer für Symbolismus in hohem Maße erfüllt. Vonnegut erschafft ein Gewebe aus Chiffren und Verweisen, das Seinesgleichen sucht. Mit den Schülerinnen und Schülern kann nur exemplarisch auf die kunstvolle Verweisstruktur eingegangen werden. Es lohnt sich aber und gehört dazu, um den literarischen Wert des Romans zu verstehen. Vorarbeit für das fragend-entwickelnde Unterrichtsgespräch wurde mit dem Ausfüllen des den Unterricht begleitenden Arbeitsblattes zu den wiederkehrenden Motiven und Symbolen geleistet (vgl. ***Copy 1, symbolism and recurring motifs, S. 36***).

1. What particular purpose does Billy as a Tralfamadorian prophet serve Vonnegut?

   Billy is a messenger of the philosophy of equanimity and calmness. He is Vonnegut's mouthpiece for proclaiming: "No more war."

2. What else does Vonnegut "owe" to the Tralfamadorians? Remember the preface and what he said about composing the novel in Chapter One.

   He says that the only way to describe "massacre" was in the "telepathic, schizophrenic" style of the Tralfamadorians.

3. Define that style. Refer to what we have just learnt about their literature.

Die Ergebnisse werden an der Tafel gesichert:

The Tralfamadorian Style

The Tralfamadorian "telegraphic, schizophrenic manner of tales is the only way to describe "massacre"	Vonnegut's realization:
• It uses telegrams and clumps of	montage structure; dissolution of chronology and linear structure
symbols	frequent repetitions of motifs, colours, symbols, and cross-references
• There must be messages	clear messages: no more war, the value of a life…
• It shows everything at the same time • Everything is read at the same time	The fragmented structure creates the illusion of simultaneity of events.

Use your list of symbols (*Copy 1, Lösungen Copy 2*) and pick some examples for the use of the cross-references.

Die Schülerinnen und Schüler können die Symbole und Motive, die auf dem Arbeitsblatt vorgegeben sind, nach Belieben wählen oder auch eigene "Funde" einbringen.

What do you think is the function of these cross-references?

Vielleicht merken die Schülerinnen und Schüler nicht von sich aus, wie sehr diese Technik zum Zusammenhalt der Lebensepisoden beiträgt. Dass es sich um eine wohlüberlegte und konstruierte Verweistechnik, die auch als Verfahren der „koordinierenden Analogien" bezeichnet wird[1], handelt, kann an zwei ausgewählten Stellen gemeinsam nachvollzogen werden. Besonders hoch ist der Gehalt an Symbolen und dergleichen zu Beginn von Kapitel fünf, der „Kidnapping"- Szene. Die Atmosphäre, die vor Billys Entführung herrscht, sein Warten, werden beklemmend unheimlich, dadurch dass Vonnegut uns mit unbewussten Assoziationen beeinflusst. Die Schülerinnen und Schüler sollen die Seiten 72–75 noch einmal genauer auf den symbolischen Gehalt hin überprüfen und die Stellen sammeln:

Let's explore one text passage that is very dense with such cross-references. Find these and interpret them by drawing a conclusion from the other contexts where you found them.

Folgende Textstellen können besprochen und mit der Deutung z. B. für die Szenenatmosphäre, die sich aus der Zusammenschau mit den Symbolen in den anderen Kontexten ergibt, an der Tafel festgehalten werden:

[1] Kuppels, Dominik: *Krieg und „schwarzer Humor". Postmoderne Erzählverfahren bei Joseph Heller (Catch-22), Kurt Vonnegut (Slaughterhouse-five) und Thomas Pynchon (Gravity's rainbow).* Tectum, Marburg 1997 (= Edition Wissenschaft; Reihe Anglistik 16; Der Begriff der „Chiffre" könnte m. E. auch zum Tragen kommen. Nach der Definition von Wilpert finden sich mannigfache „verschlüsselte Zeichen", wie z. B. der Mond. Vor allem die Farben haben diese Funktion u.v.a.m. (Gero v. Wilpert, *Sachwörterbuch der Literatur*, Kröner, Stuttgart, 1951) Für den Schulunterricht mag eine solche Differenzierung aber zu speziell sein.

The effect of cross-references

- p. 72, line 4: the tent and stripes orange and black → occurs when people are together in a kind of private harmony → quite positive
- p. 72 line 5: they nestled like spoons → used when people are actually lying in bed together and enjoying each other's warmth; a "spoonful" of syrup makes Derby happy → positive association overweighing the ironic potential
- p. 72 line 10: There was a full moon ("moonlight" repeatedly), Dresden looked like the moon after the destruction, the moon signifies Valencia's infertility → a bad signal
- p. 72 line 14: (feet) They were ivory and blue → 1st mentioning
  → Billy knows he was about to be kidnapped by a flying saucer (line 16)
  → Billy was guided by dread and the lack of dread (p. 73, line 3 ff.)
- p. 73 line 13: (the drunk on the phone) smell of his breath – mustard gas and roses.
- p. 73 line 18: blue and ivory feet → see below
- p. 74 line 25: So it goes → clear marker of death
- p. 75 line 15: his blue and ivory feet → 3 times mentioned! Always used with people who were going to die → Billy is in great danger!
- p. 75 line 29: somewhere a dog barked → announces or "comments" violence in several scenes → signal of danger and impending death

Die Schülerinnen und Schüler haben auch das Auftauchen des Leuchtzifferblattes dokumentiert. Hieran lässt sich der Tralfamadorianische Stil und das Herstellen von inhaltlicher Verbindung mittels Assoziation gut nachvollziehen. Die Schülerinnen und Schüler sollen es selbstständig versuchen, nachdem alle Stellen gefunden wurden (Radium dial: pp. 82, 90, 91).

Als Hausaufgabe kann die Interpretation schriftlich erfolgen, nachdem kurz geklärt wurde, was ein „radium dial" ist.

What about the "radium dial" on your handouts?
What is a radium dial? Write a short interpretation of its symbolical function.

The radium dial first occurs when Billy recounts his childhood. His parents had taken him on a journey to the Carlsbad Caverns. Inside the cave, it was very dark, and Billy was very afraid. The situation was horrible, and he could hardly bear the darkness when suddenly the radio dial on his father's watch shone in the darkness. For Billy it was like the light of salvation; he was saved by his father and relieved. The event remained in his memory as frightening, however. The second time the word appears it is attributed to the face of Russian soldiers. Now these fellow POWs don't really do anything active. But one of them smiles comfortingly at Billy and he reminds Billy of them being humans. That Russian somehow spreads the feeling of hope in Billy. "The Russian did not wave or speak, but he looked directly into Billy's soul with sweet hopefulness …" (p. 82). The symbolic meaning becomes obvious only much later when we learn that Billy Pilgrim was saved by the Russians. As his father saved him from the terrifying darkness and fear of death, the Russians saved Billy from the war (p. 198). This connection is indicated by the noticeable repetition of the words on the opposing pages of our text edition referring to the childhood experience and the Russians (pp. 90–91). Once these analogies have been detected, they reveal the connectivity of the symbols in the story and their function. Associations that produce connections in the reader's mind are created.

Das Buch lebt von solchen Analogien und Querverweisen. Weitere Textpassagen aus der obigen Zusammenstellung können noch gelesen und besprochen werden. Dann kann sich der Unterricht einer vergnüglicheren Sache zuwenden, dem Gebrauch des *black humours* als weiteres literarisches Gestaltungsmittels des markanten Tons des Anti-Kriegsromans.

Black Humour

Wir haben schon im ersten Kapitel Vonneguts satirischen Stil kennengelernt. Das ganze Buch ist geprägt von diesem ironischen Stil und gewollten Entgleisungen ins Vulgäre oder Obszöne, wobei auch dies auf eher humoristischer Ebene bleibt, wie z. B. der „biologische Kommentar zu Billys Sex mit Valencia: „ He had just emptied his seminal vesicles into Valencia, had contributed his share of the Green Beret. According to the Tralfamadorians, of course, the Green Beret would have seven parents in all." (pp. 118) Die Absurdität des Wirklichen wird dadurch umso plastischer. Die Schülerinnen und Schüler sollen den „schwarzen Humor" Vonneguts anhand ausgewählter Stellen definieren und seine Funktion als Stilmittel, seine Wirkung, die durchaus zu Aufregung in der Rezeption des Werkes geführt hat, kennenlernen und verstehen.

Nach der Betrachtung der Sprache auf ihren symbolischen Gehalt hin soll der ironische Stil definiert werden:

Besides the symbolical language that Vonnegut uses, as we have seen so far, do you find another stylistic feature that marks his tone?

Erwartet wird, dass das Stichwort „comic" oder "irony" fällt und dies nun genauer erarbeitet werden kann.

What kind of comical situations/ironical situations do you remember?

Es gibt viele Möglichkeiten, hier Beispiele zu nennen. Die Textpassagen können im Unterrichtsgespräch kursorisch behandelt werden, z. B.:

Billy's description as a "filthy flamingo" (pp. 24, 33, 34); Billy's tipsy search for the steering wheel in the back of the car after the comical "bit on the side" at the party (pp. 46–47); Weary kicking Billy stopped by the Germans (p. 51), "mopping-up, a postcoital satisfaction" (p. 52); Billy's only weapon: a pencil stub (p. 54); "Wild Bob"; the English POWs in their prison-paradise there: setting his coat on fire and suffering from a heartburn in the propagandist's speech (pp. 92 ff); Trout's appearance especially at the wedding anniversary – note that he is the only one without glasses (p. 170 ff.); Valencia's hysterical and finally fatal car ride to the hospital (pp. 182–183); Billy suffering from "echolalia" (p. 192); Billy's abduction by the Tralfamadorians who are thieves, by the way (p. 112); and their assumption that he is a splendid specimen (p. 113); the Tralfamadorian Zoo; the fact that they have millions of books on microfilms but no projector to show them to Billy (p. 87); Edgar Derby as the overall "ironical climax"; the bird and its "poo-tee-weet" as the most ironic comment on the meaning of life.

Viele einzelne Zeilen mit komisch-ironischem Schlagabtausch oder Assoziationsgehalt lassen sich nennen. So birgt allein die Tatsache tragische Komik, dass Billy Pilgrim, der alles andere als heldenhaft ist, aus „Ilium" stammt. „Ilium" ist eine andere Bezeichnung für das sagenhafte Troja. Den symbolischen Zusammenhang muss man aber den Schülerinnen und Schüler, so man will, erklären.

Aus der Besprechung wird eine allgemeine Bestimmung möglich, die in Stichworten an der Tafel gesichert werden kann.

> What kind of humour is it?
>
> Vonnegut uses black humour. He makes us laugh so we do not cry in situations that are almost unbearable. The irony he uses creates a tone that is serious and mocking at the same time. It moderates situations of agony and despair and works as "comic relief" where we meet pure horror or an individualized hell. It is a constant mocking tone that serves as a medium to emphasize the absurdity of it all. You could also call it "gallows humour".

Stichwörter für die Tafel:

Vonnegut's black humour

- irony, sarcasm, and comic relief
- moderation of agony, individualized hell, horror, and despair
- constant mocking tone
- serves as a medium to emphasize the absurdity of the situations

Die nächste Frage ist bewusst recht offen. Die Schülerinnen und Schüler können in Partnerarbeit ihre Gedanken sammeln und schriftlich festhalten. Die Aufgabe eignet sich auch als schriftliche Hausaufgabe:

> Why do you think he employs this style?
>
> It is in a way a "telegraphic, schizophrenic" style in language as well as in structure. He gives the message of absurdity and conveys – schizophrenically – the idea of "the good in the bad". Such ambiguity is produced by the language.
> The ironic style used is optimal to describe the absolute irony of fate that Vonnegut experienced: his life was endangered down there in the "meat locker" of the Slaughterhouse-Five in Dresden not by his enemy, the Germans, but by his own people. The bombs were thrown by the Americans and their allies! The former "meat locker" almost turns into that room of stocking dead bodies again. The real enemy has gone home in the meantime. He will find death as well but absurdly not on the battlefield but at home in the seemingly secure environment of his family. The real irony of life has led to the use of irony in Vonnegut's writing and it sometimes turns into more bitter sarcasm, and sometimes into comic parody, creating Vonnegut's particular brand of black humour.

Die Aufmerksamkeit der Schülerinnen und Schüler wird zusätzlich auf Vonneguts Inspiration für die Technik gelenkt:

1. Is there another reason apart from the "Tralfamadorian style model" that might account for the "black humour"? What does Vonnegut say about the real emergence of literature?

   Vonnegut was very much influenced by reading Erika Ostrovsky's *Celine and His Vision* (pp. 20–21). He got the motivation for some of his ideas from there and he points out Celine's concept of art: "No art is possible without a dance with death." So, literature, as an art form, also falls into this category. Celine then wrote "grotesque novels". Here we can perceive another meaning of the story's third title: it not only refers to real death as it occurs in Dresden and the war. It is Vonnegut's connotation of the style he uses in the book: the humourous, comical, ironic language creates such lightness that even the atrocious, horrible scenes dance by in the chain of life. Life seems to be a crazy round dance, going on and on for generations of humans, always repeating the same cycle: birth, the struggle to survive, and finally death – all of this signifying – perhaps – nothing.

2. Can you guess why quite a lot of people found the book a detestable blasphemy because of its language?

   A lot of irony is used in parts where Christianity or American society is mentioned. People might be offended by the rude language, for example that of Roland Weary and especially Lazzaro, e.g. "'People fuck up with me,' he said, 'and Jesus Christ are they ever fucking sorry'" (p. 139). Vonnnegut uses rude language to express his criticism and rejection of religion, e.g. the passage on Kilgore Trout's *The Gospel from Outer space*, where he calls Jesus a "nobody" and a "bum" adopted by God as his son (pp. 108ff.). He also criticises warfare and middle class hypocrisy e.g. the "naturalist" description of Billy about to urinate, "Billy took his pecker out", p. 124.

Auf die Rezeption und kontroverse Aufnahme des Romans bis hin zu seinem noch heute andauernden Verbot an manchen Schulen wird nachfolgend eingegangen. Zunächst ergibt sich aus der erwähnten tragi-komischen Darstellung Billys seine Funktion als Antiheld.

7.2 The anti-hero Billy Pilgrim and the tragic hero Edgar Derby

In der Gegenüberstellung mit dem martialischen Roland Weary wurde klar, dass Billy Pilgrim alles andere als der geborene, enthusiastische Krieger ist (vgl. 5.1 Billy Pilgrim and Roland Weary). Vonnegut schuf mit ihm einen klassischen Antihelden, den er zum Protagonisten macht, obwohl er selbst im ersten Kapitel erwähnt, dass eigentlich Edgar Derby der tragische Held der Geschichte sei.
Ausgehend von der Definition des Anti-Helden und der Charakterisierung Edgar Derbys als tragische Figur soll ermittelt werden, warum Vonnegut dem schwachen Charakter den Vorzug gibt. Dabei zeigt es sich, dass der Krieg als Verbrechen am Menschen besonders durch das Kindhafte an Billy angeprangert wird. Er ist daher für die „message" des Autors besser geeignet als die Figur des schon älteren, robusten Lehrers.

1. Can you define what an "anti-hero" is?

   An anti-hero is a character in fiction who is the opposite of the traditional strong and glorious hero. He is weak, lacks skill, is clumsy, a fool, or a person with a weak and instable character. He might also be burdened with illness and bad luck. Moreover, he shows cowardice and a lack of valour and dignity in tense situations.

2. Billy Pilgrim is said to be a classic anti-hero. Can you support this from what you know about him? Use the characteristics we have already determined about him and find passages from the text that prove this statement.

Die Ergebnisse an der Tafel oder auf dem OHP:

Billy Pilgrim – the classic anti-hero

1. Outer appearance:

- He is described as a"flamingo, clown, scarecrow, and a box of kitchen matches".
- He looks like a transvestite in the funny coat, ridiculous, bobbing up and down with his broken shoe, like a drunkard.
- With his blue toga, he is a real laughing-stock. A woman working in the slaughter-house-kitchen is stunned and diagnoses from his appearance that all the heroic warriors must be dead if now such children in costumes come to war.

2. Behaviour:

- He is slow; Roland Weary has to drag him along behind the German lines.
- He is lethargic and weary of life; he wants to die on the battlefield and be left alone by Weary and the scouts.
- He behaves like an intimidated and inexperienced youngster: he is embarrassed by the rude word "motherfucker" and the naked girls in Dresden and he believes in animal magnetism.
- As a child, he is afraid of water, darkness, and Jesus on the cross.

3. Actions:

- Most of the time, he is rather passive, causes anger or stumbles into trouble.
- He gets lost behind enemy lines with no weapons or other useful equipment.
- He stumbles through the snow like a drunken or foolish person.
- He causes the "Three Musketeers" to break up.
- He disturbs the prisoners' sleep.
- He causes Weary unnecessary pain when bumping into him on the march with Weary suffering from bleeding feet from which he will die in the end.
- He sets himself on fire, watching the "Cinderella musical" in the Englishmen's camp.

4. Others take advantage of him:

- He has to work as a dumper of the POW's excrements on the boxcar.
- Reporters snatch him and throw him into bushes to take a photo of a live capture. Because he looks so fantastically inept, Billy, as a ridiculous wreck, presents the American soldiers awkwardly.
- Others get good military coats while he gets a woman's garment. One of the English POWs even accuses him of being a humiliation for his troop.

Anhand dieser Tatsachen ist das Bild des Antihelden Billy Pilgrim gut erfasst. Es soll durch einige markante Aussagen zu seiner generell pessimistischen Einstellung zum Leben und seinem schlichten kindlichen Gemüt abgerundet werden:

What do we additionally learn about Billy's attitude towards life?

He is a pessimist and a rather frustrated person. The narrator's comment on his childhood and relationship to his father and especially mother are commented with the short but clear sentence: "Billy didn't like life at all" (p. 102). Lost behind the German lines, he would rather the others leave him alone then struggle for survival. He does not cling to life very much.

Die als Beispiel genannte Passage kann angelesen werden (pp. 136–137), nachdem die Frage gestellt wurde:

What does the fact that Billy does not immediately take out the two lumps in his coat tell you about his mindset? (pp. 136–137)

He is said to believe in "animal magnetism". This is a rather strange attitude and almost childlike, believing in wonders, magic, and fairy tales. He might believe they are a kind of good luck charm. But this just reveals that his mind is puerile and totally out of place in the adult reality of war.

Die folgenden Fragen können im Unterrichtsgespräch behandelt werden. Die Schlussfolgerung kann als Hausaufgabe schriftlich gesichert werden und das Fazit dann an der Tafel festgehalten werden.

1. Would you consider Billy Pilgrim an "anti-hero" throughout the novel? What about his professional career as an optometrist after the war? Isn't he a good family man as well?

   Things would be fine if it hadn't been for his time travelling. So he is never really ahead of his affairs and never has sovereign control of his life. Another feature of the anti-hero that was mentioned was being beaten down by bad luck. Billy has a lot of this happening to him: the plane crash and Valencia's death, for example.

2. A hero is usually a clever and intelligent person. As such, he or she learns from mistakes. Can you make any statement about Billy in this respect?

   Billy is so proud of his son who turns from a difficult child into a shiny Green Beret soldier (p. 121). We would have expected him to do as the author-narrator did: never ever to let that happen, after all his experiences in war. He warns his sons to keep away from it (p. 19). But Billy takes the Vietnam war for granted, as something that has to happen. He does not take a stand in the Lions Club whose president he is and where propaganda in favour of this war is being made. He has learnt nothing (pp. 59 ff.). This is not only a pity but again a sign of his weakness in character and mind. This is also exactly the tone of his comment on how the war was for him when Valencia once asks him. She wants to know if it was awful. His answer is "sometimes" (p. 121), so that we get the impression that the whole impact has not really been felt in his consciousness – whether this is because of repression or a lack of intelligence. He seems not to have become wiser.

3. In conclusion: why then did Vonnegut choose an anti-hero for his book?

   A person like Billy Pilgrim undermines our ordinary concept of a soldier. Finding this childlike fool placed in the middle of war seems so absolutely wrong that the reader must become aware of the injustice of war and its contempt for human life. The fact that such inept persons are sent out to war also throws a bad light on the whole system and machinery of the military apparatus and the idea of war as a means to solve political problems. It is the real and innocent human being who must suffer and die on behalf of ideological considerations that he or she might even not be able to comprehend. Billy Pilgrim is the embodiment of a victim in more than one sense. He is the embodiment of the moral injustice of sending the innocent to war like cattle to the slaughterer's.

Die Schlussfolgerung kann entweder nach der Bearbeitung im Unterricht oder nach dem Besprechen der als Hausaufgabe erstellten Texte an der Tafel festgehalten werden:

The function of Billy Pilgrim as an anti-hero

Billy Pilgrim's anti-hero status functions as a moral comment on the injustice of sending the innocent to war like cattle to the slaughterhouse.

Comparing Billy Pilgrim to Edgar Derby

Durch den Vergleich mit der Funktion Edgar Derbys wird die Bedeutung des Antihelden Billy Pilgrims für Vonneguts Kritik am Krieg noch stärker. Dazu soll Derbys Geschichte rekonstruiert werden:

1. Although Vonnegut declared Edgar Derby as the real hero of his story in the first chapter, he chose the weak character Billy Pilgrim as the protagonist. Let's explore why he did not choose Derby in the first place.

2. How does the reader meet Edgar Derby?

   Edgar Derby is mentioned before Billy Pilgrim in the first chapter. He is already the declared tragic figure of the story and his futile death will be the climax of it. He is indirectly introduced and always referred to as the old, poor, or even doomed Edgar Derby (cf. p. 92).

Für die nächste Aufgabe muss eventuell die Erklärung zum sprechenden Namen "Derby" gegeben werden, wenn die Schülerinnen und Schüler nicht von selbst darauf kommen. Oder man bringt ein einsprachiges Wörterbuch mit und lässt eine Schülerin oder einen Schüler die Bedeutungen vorlesen. Edgar Derby ist den Schülerinnen und Schüler schon bei der Besprechung von Billy Pilgrims Kriegserlebnissen begegnet und wurde im Beziehungstrapez als die Person identifiziert, die eigentlich allen nur wohl will. Er ist der väterliche „Kümmerer" und soll aus der Beschreibung als d e r aufrichtige Charakter hervortreten. Nach Vorstellung der Aufgabe können die Schülerinnen und Schüler in Partnerarbeit entsprechende Textstellen aufsuchen. Im Unterrichtsgespräch können diese Kernstellen angelesen und besprochen werden. Eine schriftliche Zusammenfassung kann in Einzelarbeit im Unterricht oder zu Hause erfolgen:

1. Edgar Derby bears a "telling name" as well as Billy or other persons in the story. A "derby" can mean two things. Either it denotes a hat that is also known as a bowler. This is a hard black hat with a curved brim and round top, very typical for business men in Britain in the past. Or it is also a sports competition. A demolition derby is a stock car race, for example.
2. Use this information in your summary of Edgar Derby's story. Collect the information from the book and your reading companions with your work partner.
3. Write an essay of at least 250 words. Do this alone as homework.
4. Point out what makes Edgar Derby special among the other characters.

Mögliche Stichwörter zur Erstellung des Aufsatzes während des Unterrichtsgespräches an der Tafel :

Edgar Derby – the tragic hero

"telling name" → "old-fashioned hat":
out-moded model of ideals like patriotism, civil courage, responsibility, caring for others, and the glory of war
→ sports competition: fairness, fitness of the body and mind

Age: 44 /45 years old

Profession: teacher ("Contemporary Problems in Western Civilization")

Hobby: tennis team coach

Family: father of a son fighting in Vietnam. He loves his wife.

Interests: politics. He is a fervent patriot and believes in the American system.

Citation: "But old Derby was a character now" (p. 164).

Fate: pure irony! He survives the Dresden bombing but is executed for minor theft, the stealing of a teapot (p. 105).

Musteraufsatz:

Edgar Derby's last name reminds one of the dome-shaped hats worn by some elderly men, the "Derby", which was fashionable during World War II. So from that telling name, one can immediately assume that "poor old Edgar Derby", as he is often referred to, is an "out-dated model" of a character. "Patriotism, middle age and imaginary wisdom" are the attributes that are attached to him (p. 150). But he is also described as "one of the best bodies" and is a high school teacher from Indianapolis, who had taught "Contemporary Problems in Western Civilization". He had coached the tennis team and was in good shape for a 44-year-old father of a son, who was fighting as a marine in the Pacific (p. 83).
He is a caring, well-natured person. He cradled Weary in his arms when he died in the boxcar (p. 83) and sat at Billy's bed when he was given a shot of morphine and put in the prison hospital (p. 98). He is the one who verbalizes the insight that the war was a children's crusade when the English colonel asks him why he and Billy didn't shave (p. 106).
Derby believed in the cause of war and had even volunteered. He does not shy away from responsibility but, like a "father", takes on the role of the speaker for

the POWs. As a teacher, he is able to deliver a speech as the leader of the American POWs fluently and takes his job seriously (p. 146). He is politically interested and courageously speaks his mind in Dresden when the American Nazi Howard W. Campbell, Jr., holds his recruiting speech in front of the prisoners, holding American ideals in contempt.
Edgar Derby is t h e character. Vonnegut points out that "one of the main effects of war … [was] that people [were] discouraged from being characters. But old Derby was a character now" (p. 164). He is the outstanding, morally upright character. But fate will have it that this outstanding, decent, and honest man will die a pointless death: he will be sentenced to death by a sudden improvised summary court for alleged plundering. He will take a teapot from the wreckage after the bombing and therefore be shot by a firing squad on the spot (p. 83; p. 214).

Was will Vonnegut mit Edgar Derbys unsinnigem Tod zeigen? Im Partnergespräch sollen die Schülerinnen und Schüler eine Antwort darauf finden und in wenigen Sätzen formulieren:

1. What does Vonnegut want to show us with Edgar Derby's death?

   Edgar Derby's death is *the* prime example for the absurdity and injustice of war. He suffers an untimely death in absurd circumstances: Derby survived the bombing of Dresden and all the battlefield hardship but got executed for a minor theft. He is a victim of bad luck and the lack of flexibility, common sense, and humanity of a system that ignores its own doomed fate. War creates exceptional cases of the cruel and absurd demise of the individual and of insane contempt for one's fellow human beings.

2. Compare Billy Pilgrim to Edgar Derby. Why did Vonnegut prefer Billy Pilgrim as his main protagonist after all?

   Edgar Derby is a kind of "finished" or complete character and copes with life fairly well. He has volunteered to serve in the army and is always in control of his feelings and actions. Therefore, he is not so interesting for readers. Although he attracts our compassion, we feel much more drawn to the puerile Billy Pilgrim. This is especially so because we are already directed towards his story because of the author's denouncement of the "children's crusade". Billy is bestowed with the strange ability to travel in time. That wouldn't have worked with Edgar Derby; it wouldn't have been congruent with his character and mindset. But even if he is not the main protagonist, as he could have been according to the author-narrator, he has a fundamental function in sharpening Billy Pilgrim's role as the anti-hero.
   In contrast with Derby's character, Billy looks even more like the lost, disoriented boy who needs caring for and is absolutely inept. Billy Pilgrim can only step out of the novel as the anti-hero and model of the innocent human being abused by the mechanisms and mongerings of war so impressively because of the counter-character of the "better man" – Edgar Derby. What – if any sense – does a war make if it is not those who are physically and mentally fit for the battle but the "Cinderella" of the story who survives in the end?

Wir erfahren, dass sich Edgar Derby ständig mit der Absicht trägt, Briefe nach Hause zu senden. Er formuliert sie im Kopf, aber er kommt nie dazu, sie zu Papier zu bringen. Die Schülerinnen und Schüler sollen einen Brief an seine Frau nach Hause erfinden. Die Aufgabe kann zu Hause erfüllt werden.

Write Edgar Derby's letter home to his wife (cf. p. 143).

Der Brief kann außer Beschreibungen seiner Verfassung, der Begegnung mit Billy und den anderen auch seine Wahl zum Lagersprecher und sein mutiges Auftreten gegenüber Campbell, dem Propagandamacher, zum Inhalt haben.

7. 3 The absurdity of war

Social Darwinism and religion

Der Vergleich von Billy Pilgrim mit Edgar Derby führt vor Augen, wie Krieg zum einen unbarmherzig mit den Individuen verfährt. Zum anderen legt er den Widersinn der brutalen Gewaltaktion offen, denn es sind nicht die, die am besten dafür trainiert, gerüstet oder sonst wie ausgestattet sind, auch nicht die, die mit „Hurrah" in die Schlacht ziehen, wie Roland Weary, es sind gerade eben auch die Schwachen, tumben Gestalten, oder wie im Falle von Lazzaro, sogar die kriminellen Perversen, die den Irrsinn überleben. Darwins Idee des „survival of the fittest" als die Überlebensstrategie der Spezies, scheint damit als Lüge überführt. Aber mitnichten setzt Vonnegut Darwin außer Kraft: können aus einem von Menschen der eigenen Spezies aufgezwungenen widernatürlichen Zustand der Gewalt und der Menschenverachtung nicht tatsächlich nur solche Gestalten hervorgehen? Ist hier nicht tatsächlich der apathisch-schizophrene mit Gleichmut erduldende Charakter, oder der listig-durchtriebene, gewaltbereite der am besten Ausgestattete?
In Kapitel 10 spitzt sich genau dieser Widerspruch durch die geballte Ansammlung von Gegensätzen zum Höhepunkt der Kritik am Wahnsinn Krieg zu. Die Morde an Robert Kennedy und Dr. Martin Luther King, der Tod des Vaters, die Unmenschlichkeit der Leichenzählung in Vietnam werden mit dem Spaziergang Billys durch den Frühling scharf kontrastiert. Die Verbindung zwischen den gewaltsamen Toden und Billy liegt in der Tatsache, dass auch Billy von einem „sniper" erschossen wird. Damit wird er quasi in den Rang der wichtigen Männer erhoben, auch sein Schicksal ist ein beachtenswertes. Gleichzeitig ist eben dies der Anlass, wiederum über den „Wert" des menschlichen Lebens nachzudenken.
Vonnegut erwähnt dazu auch die Begegnung mit dem Maori in diesem Kapitel. Eine Absurdität, wie sie nur Billy Pilgrim begegnen kann: Da arbeitet mit ihm in den Leichenbergen dieser neuseeländische Eingeborene, der in Libyen (Toburk) gefangen genommen worden war, und dieser Bär von einem Mann stirbt – nicht im Kampf, nicht durch die Bomben – sondern weil er sich im wahrsten Sinne des Wortes „Lunge und Leber" durch den Verwesungsgestank erbricht!
Wie Derby ist er ein Stellvertreter für die biologisch und physisch überlegenen Exemplare der Gattung – aber ein kleiner Billy Pilgrim erträgt mit stoischer Gelassenheit auch dies und ergibt sich auch in dieses abscheuliche Schicksal. Der mit den am wenigsten außergewöhnlichen oder ruhmvollen Fähigkeiten überlebt, wandelt durch den Frühling und hört die Vöglein singen. Welcher Hohn!
Die Schülerinnen und Schüler sollen anhand des letzten Kapitels das oben angesprochene Thema der auf den Kopf gestellten Evolutionstheorie erkennen. Billy zeichnet sich durch nichts außer durch seinen Gleichmut aus. Diesen hat er sich einerseits bewahrt , andererseits wurde er darin durch die Tralfamadorianer bestärkt. Für sein Überleben spielt dabei die Religion eine immer unwichtigere Rolle. Der Tralfamadorianische Fatalismus ersetzt die Religion und Gott, versöhnt Billy Pilgrim mit sich und der Welt.

Das 10. Kapitel lässt sich sehr gut ganz mit der CD rezipieren. Die Schülerinnen und Schüler können den Text mitlesen (CD 5, Track 6, 9:52 min).
Der Leseauftrag lautet, zunächst den Inhalt kurz in eigenen Worten wiederzugeben. Danach geht es um den Eindruck, der durch die Kontrastierung der wie Kugeln aus dem Gewehr

schnell aneinanderhektographierten, furchtbaren historischen Morde und Billys Frühlingserleben entsteht:

1. Read along and then give a short summary of the chapter. What impression does it make on you? Does anything strike you as being odd?

   There is an obvious juxtaposition of the horrible historical murders and Billy's walk through the streets in spring, as if in a dream. The singing of the bird adds to the absurd atmosphere, seeming to say "don't worry, everything is over: you will be fine now. Grass will grow over everything." That is almost surreal or like dream walking.

2. Why do you think spring is the season for Billy's walk?

   Spring is the symbol of new life. Billy has survived. He can start anew.

3. We have talked about Billy and Edgar Derby and the idea of who, theoretically, would have better "deserved" to survive. Do you see any parallel to this idea in this chapter?

   A Maori is mentioned. Like Edgar Derby, he is physically better suited for warfare than Billy Pilgrim but he dies because he cannot bear the stench of the decaying bodies.

4. So who are the survivors?

   They are not necessarily the fittest of the species.

5. Isn't that a contradiction to the Darwinian law of evolution?

Die Diskussion sollte Vonneguts Absicht, die Perversion von Krieg zu untermauern, auf den Punkt bringen und könnte in den Tafelanschrieb münden:

The survival of the fittest and war

The survival of the fittest = Charles Darwin's theory of evolution (all species develop through natural selection based on the ability to survive and reproduce; *On the Origin of Species*, 1859)

Social Darwinism
- The survival of the fittest within the social system, rules, institutions and so on, normally in peaceful times. The selection follows the rules of evolution.
- Warfare and Darwinism (according to Vonnegut)
- Modern warfare does not reject the unsuitable, weak, inept species for survival; it does not necessarily prefer the biologically, physically and psychologically fittest. The selection is unjust and often absurd.

1. The author-narrator tells us that the Tralfamadorians were not so much interested in Jesus Christ but in Charles Darwin instead (p. 210). Can you guess why?

   They understand Darwin's theory in reverse: he said the best will survive. They put it this way: Darwin said the unsuited will die. The improvement of

the species is due to the bad material sorted out by death. This is no doubt true according to Darwin. This is something that they can directly observe and explore.
They attribute importance only to things and events that they have explored scientifically. So they might have perceived the phenomenon of Jesus Christ as something as singular as the idea of "Free Will" that they only found with the human race. Compared to the amount of universal data they have, these terrestrial phenomena are of minute significance. They are more interested in natural science that has empirical quality. They might also conclude from their observations that religion, as something that cannot be measured in physical quality in terms of its effects, has no visible impact on the survival strategies of the human race. These strategies seem to be the pre-eminent point of interest regarding humans for them.

2. Billy Pilgrim started as an assistant to a chaplain. Why do you think Vonnegut did not, according to his own biography, simply make him an ordinary soldier?

Die Antwort leitet die Diskussion darüber ein, dass Vonnegut Kritik an der Verbindung von Religion und Krieg übt. In Gruppenarbeit soll nach den einschlägigen Textpassagen gesucht und eine Gesamtdarstellung der Thematik erarbeitet werden.

1. What does Vonnegut say about religion and war in the novel? Research this in groups.
2. Find examples from the text to show how religion is dealt with.
3. Explain why it is dealt with in this way.
4. What is the author's intention?

Die Gruppen (4– 6 Schülerinnen und Schüler) erhalten ca. 20 Minuten Zeit. Jede Gruppe soll jemanden zum Schreiben und Präsentieren bestimmen. Die Ergebnisse werden auf Folien, die in die Gruppen gegeben werden, gesichert und anschließend auf dem Projektor vorgestellt. Die Ergebnisse können in eine thematische Ordnung gebracht werden. Z. B. können folgende Textstellen exemplarisch herausgegriffen werden:

Religion in Slaughterhouse-Five

1 Billy's religious belief:

- His mother has made him believe in God and go to church. He sings hymns and prayers and plays the organ. They are Protestants. His father had no religion (p. 38).

2. Futility of hoping for help from "above":

- Billy was a chaplain's assistant in the American Army, a valet to a preacher with a meek faith in a loving Jesus, that the other soldiers loathe (p. 30–31).
- Right from the start, his training in the Californian manoeuvres is mocked by the comment on the troop's failure, "They were all theoretically dead now", while Billy was playing "A Mighty Fortress Is Our God". The futility of faith in God is already alluded to (p. 31).

3. Billy seems to be a reincarnation of Jesus:

- There are several allusions to Billy and Jesus:
  - Although Billy was not a Catholic, his mother hung up a "ghastly crucifix" in his room that he

found extremely gruesome (p. 38–39). His mother seems to have been foreseeing his fate. It is as if she wanted to tell him, "Look he has endured suffering, so will you."

- In the boxcar, Billy's sleeping position is described as "self-crucified" (p. 80).
- The most direct allusion to Jesus is made when the reason for the Chrismas carol is revealed (p. 197).

4. Derision of biblical stories and Christianity and the use of blasphemous language:

- The topic of religion and God's role in the war is treated in a sarcastic and even blasphemous way, for example:
  - "The gun made a ripping sound like the opening of the zipper on the fly of God Almighty" (p. 34).
  - "Billy stared into the patina of the corporal's boots, saw Adam and Eve in the golden depth. They were naked. They were innocent..."; "Billy looked up at the face ...The boy was as beautiful as Eve" (p. 53).
  - "The corporal reached into Weary's gaping bosom as though he meant to tear out his pounding heart, but he brought out Weary's bullet-proof Bible instead. A bullet-proof Bible is ..."(p. 54). Note the immediate mentioning of the pornographic pony+photo that the corporal finds in the hip-pocket. (Heart – Bible; lower body+region+porno+picture) (p. 55).
  - It is Christmas when Billy is on the boxcar nestling with fellow prisoners and doing his humiliating job of dumping everybody's excrements (p. 71).
  - The treatment of the latrines as a kind of "religious ceremony", keeping them clean and using them as a place of individual retreat for self-reflection is a great blow in the face of religion. It is the place where Billy dives into deeper thought about the sense of life. The scene is rendered even more sarcastic by the sudden appearance of the author-narrator who comments that he had just "excremented his brains as well". So how and why think about the meaning of it all. There is none. (p. 124–125)
  - "Leave the latrine as tidy as you found it!" (p. 125). The scene also matches with the image of "God's zipper" (cf. p. 34). Billy is contemplating life while peeing (p. 124).
  - The most provocative direct attacks against religion are to be found in the books of Kilgore Trout. Remarkably, the issue of Jesus or religion is never directly discussed by Billy and only related as citations of that fictional writer, for example:
  - In *The Gospel from Outer Space*, the extra-terrestrial visitor makes a serious study of Christianity to find out why Christians found it so easy to be cruel: "The gospels actually taught this: Before you kill somebody, make absolutely sure he isn't well connected," (p. 108–109).
  - "The visitor from outer space made a gift to Earth of a new Gospel. In it, Jesus really was a nobody, and a pain in the neck to a lot of people ..." (p. 109–110).
  - "Another Kilgore Trout book [...] was about a man who built a time machine so he could go back and see Jesus [...] It was a cross [...] Jesus and his father had built it [...]. And the rabble-rouser was executed on it" (p. 202).
  - "The time-traveler in the book went back to Bible times to find out ... whether or not Jesus had really died on the cross...The hero had a stethoscope along. ... The Son of God was dead as a doornail" (p. 203). Note that it is not Billy who does so. He never leaves his own life in his time travels.
  - The end of the universe is not in God's hand but in that of the Tralfamadorians (p. 116–117).
  - Billy and Montana, the "new Adam and Eve", are also an example with their credo of equanimity (the prayer) and function as the new parents of mankind. Billy has the prayer text on the wall of his office; Montana wears it as a pendant between her breasts.

Die Besprechung kann dann das epigrammatische Gedicht, die Verse des Weihnachtsliedes am Anfang des Buches, aufgreifen, um die Absicht des Autors daraus und aus dem Besprochenen abzuleiten. Die schriftliche Erläuterung eignet sich als Hausaufgabe:

1. Turn to the very beginning of your books. Do you remember that we wondered about the little poem on the front page?
   [The cattle are lowing,/The Baby awakes,/But the little Jesus/No crying He makes]

2. What do you think about its meaning now? Write an interpretation. Take into consideration what Vonnegut explains about his application of the verses to Billy Pilgrim.

Modellaufsatz:

The Christmas carol stands for Billy Pilgrim's attitude towards all the atrocities that happen to him during the war and even later on in life. "The cattle are lowing" stands for the tumultuous events around him, like the ordeal behind the German lines, the Dresden bombardment, the plane crash, and Valencia's death. "The Baby awakes", the second line, refers to Billy Pilgrim's realization that he has been afflicted by the circumstances but still is not fully "awake". He does not completely grasp the meaning of all that happens around him. There is no reason in all the mischief and like "the little Lord Jesus" who does not cry although he hears loud "terrifying" noises, he never complains or blames anyone for his plight. He could curse God for leaving him on his own, he could blame the Germans for taking him prisoner, or he could accuse the War Allies and his own fellow countrymen for exposing him to the bombing, to name just some examples – but he never even thinks of revenge, retribution or the like. Like Jesus, he is a silent sufferer. He accepts his lot quietly without complaining. Neither he nor Jesus could change "the present, past or the future" (p. 60).
The quatrain is repeated in Chapter 9 (p. 197) and its application to Billy Pilgrim is explained. It refers to his habit of clandestine weeping: "Later on, as a middle-aged optometrist, he would weep quietly and privately sometimes, but never make aloud boohooing noises." He is meek as a lamb and said to resemble "the Christ in the carol" in that he had also seen many things that made him cry (p. 197).
Although Billy Pilgrim is compared to Jesus, he is not heightened to a heavenly martyr character or the like. Quite the opposite. Vonnegut depicts the innocent childlike soul of a man who once had a devote faith in God but awoke from that innocent state of belief to a more sober realization that God might not really be interested in mankind.

Abschließend sollen die Schülerinnen und Schüler eine Zusammenfassung der Problematik anfertigen. Nach Besprechung der Aufgabe wird das Ergebnis in Partnerarbeit schriftlich gesichert:

Does Vonnegut reject religion? If so, does he offer an alternative?

Vonnegut's position ultimately appears to be clearly secular. He seems to be declaring Christianity to be a religion of cruelty. Evidence for this can be found in the gruesome Crucifix in Billy's room and the alien visitor's conviction that Christians are a species of extraordinary "cruelness". Vonnegut seems to be saying that religion is a soothing illusion for meek believers as long as its ideal of

humanity is not put to the test: in times of need, it does not affect anything. Wars are usually carried out with "God's blessing" for the soldiers. Roland Weary has the steel-coated Bible with him. Even these Christian fighters are not saved from death. It is the enduring tormenting question: where is God when you need him?
But Vonnegut does not blame God for being absent. Although he mocks at the Bible and even uses rude and offensive language to emphasize the uselessness of religious faith in war, he never condemns Christianity. He does not blame God for letting wars happen. He does not reject the philosophy of Christianity, but he rejects it as a truth in itself. Judging his position from the way he depicts the topic in the novel, one could call him an agnostic, neither believing in the existence of God nor denying it completely. With the creation of the Tralfamadorians, he offers an alternative to God – at least to Billy Pilgrim. Their ability to live in four dimensions and independence from time makes them creatures of eternal life and limitless knowledge.

Free Will – predestination and fatalism

Vonnegut schafft mit den Tralfamadorianern so etwas wie „Ersatzgötter". Billy wird zu ihrem Propheten.
DieTralfamadorianische Philosophie hat ihren Platz im Rahmen der Kriegskritik. An ihr zeigt sich die Dichotomie von Vorbestimmung und Willensfreiheit, die im Roman immer wieder auftritt. Es kann keine Willensfreiheit auf der Welt geben, denn wie könnten sonst vernunftbegabte Wesen Krieg wollen? Muss es den Menschen nicht vorbestimmt sein, den als Krieg „strukturierten Moment" wie den Moment des Todes eben durchleben zu müssen, weil es so bestimmt ist? Angesichts der Tatsache, dass Menschen Menschen töten, kommt Vonnegut zu diesem Schluss. Er lässt Billy Pilgrim diese nüchterne Erkenntnis durch die Tralfamadorianer machen und zu deren Sprachrohr werden.

Die Schülerinnen und Schüler sollen zunächst Billys Gelassenheitsgebet und seine Tralfamadorianische Fatalismuslehre in Einklang bringen.[1]

1. Billy seems not completely to have fallen from the Christian belief although he has stopped going to church. He even has a prayer on the wall of his office: "God grant me / The serenity to accept / The things I cannot change, / Courage / To change the things I can, / And wisdom always / To tell the Difference." Montana Wildhack even wears this prayer as a pendant around her neck. How does it relate to the Tralfamadorian principles that Billy calls himself a prophet of?

   The Tralfamadorians have taught Billy to accept things as his fate. They practise a kind of positive fatalism. Their motto is: So it goes. This means that things will always be the way they are. All events are simultaneous; they are moments structured in a way that cannot be influenced. It is the positive message they have for Billy, that men will live forever (p. 211) that calms Billy and he learns to concentrate on the good times only (pp. 194–195). Everything is predetermined, and death is just a moment in eternal life. It is nothing to be scared of but something to be accepted as one cannot change

[1] Die Begriffe der Prädestination, des freien Willens und des Fatalismus oder Existenzialismus sind hochphilosophische Konzepte, die leider im Umfang des Englischunterrichts nicht intensiv vertieft werden können. Es sei denn, man gibt die Themen als Referate auf, z.B. zu Boethius' und Aquinas Prädestinationslehre, ggf. als *Post-reading*-Beitrag.

it anyway. So there is no need to be active and rebellious; all actions are preordained before they occur. It is the idea of "predestination" that rules this conception of the world. Even Billy who is able to shift in time cannot really influence it: "Among the things Billy Pilgrim could not change were the past, the present, and the future."

There is no such thing as "Free Will": "Everything is all right, and everybody has to do exactly what he does" (p. 198). This is what he learns from the Tralfamadorians. It is a positive revelation and, for him, a better option to deal with the traumatic experiences of his childhood and as a prisoner of war and an ailing widower. By the way, the Tralfamadorians' observation is supported by their scientific explorations proving the phenomenon of "Free Will" as a singularity occurring only on the planet earth (p. 117).

2. How does Vonnegut emphasize that "Free Will" does not exist?

Obviously, Billy has no control over his time travels. He can neither determine the time when they happen, nor to what period of his life or location he will travel.
As prisoners, the men, including Billy, have no "Free Will" at all. They are not only physically restricted, but they are even actively manipulated as regards their decisions by being exposed, for example, to the Nazi propaganda of Colonel Campbell. He wants to influence them in the ideological direction of the German Hitler regime.
"Free Will" and serving in war as a soldier are absolute incompatibilities. Orders have to be followed and not reflected upon, discussed or even doubted.

Die Schülerinnen und Schüler beschäftigen sich anschließend mit der Darstellung des Krieges als solchen. Damit erfassen sie den Charakter des Romans als Anti-Kriegsroman in seiner Gänze:

Show from the text how Vonnegut presents war as inhumane and what it does to men who used to be civilized. Write an essay referring to pages 64–65 and 116–117.

Die Textstellen werden still gelesen und in Partnerarbeit entsprechend der Aufgabe bearbeitet. Die inhaltlichen Aspekte lassen sich wie folgt deuten und können als Still- oder Hausaufgabe als Essay ausformuliert werden:

Vonnegut uses the metaphor "river of humiliation" in describing the march of the captured American prisoners of war; they are led away like the"Mississippi of humiliated Americans". The worst part of this scene is that they are watched by viciously triumphant disgusting German soldiers. Their meanness is stressed by the way they are described using metaphors, e.g., "they had teeth like piano keys". The most equivocal association is evoked by relating their way of devouring sausages while sitting on top of a tank. The canon pipe can surely be imagined to be an allusion to an erect penis underlining the disgusting triumph of the enemy. The most abhorrent humiliation happens to Weary who is spat upon with "a fourragère of snot and blutwurst and tobacco", that is an ejection of that revolting substance. What an intense picture of human contempt! The devilish victors are said to have taken "wolfish bites from sausages" (p. 64). They are like wolves and this reminds us of the philosophical saying: man is a wolf to his (fellow) men or *homo homini lupus est*! Vonnegut, as a student of anthropology, knows his philosophers well and here he clearly alludes to Hob-

bes' theory of the *state of nature of man*, which is the war of man against every man. And that is exactly the state of Dresden and the world in war at the time of the Second World War.[1]
These truths are hard to admit, as hard as the summary of the earth's history of mankind that Billy delivers to the Tralfamadorians: "As you know, I am from a planet that has been engaged in senseless slaughter since the beginning of time." Hence another connotation of the title of the book, the conviction that our world is a bad one, ruled by creatures who slaughter one another; even the innocent girls, they were "boiled alive" for the sake of his own countrymen "who were proud of fighting pure evil at the time" (p. 116). Vonnegut does not mince his words and can only draw the conclusion: earthlings must be the terrors of the universe! And here the blame is on the Americans and they certainly did not like their own failure being spelt out to them so directly. Moreover, Vonnegut does not spare them the memory of Hiroshima and the atomic bomb disaster, another historical event of contemptuous behaviour towards civilian people and children.

What else might have caused people to be angry about the book, looking at Vonnegut's attitude towards the Americans and their much-loved ideal, prevalent in a large section of the American population, of themselves as the liberators of the world, sending their army around the world as a godsend?

Vonnegut claims that war is absolutely good for nothing. Or – as he points out ironically with Rosewater's assertion when Valencia proudly presents the diamond Billy had found in the coat : "That's the attractive thing about war ... Absolutely everybody gets a little something" (p. 111). So was it worth it? Surely not for Edgar Derby whose wish for a wartime souvenir, the teapot, cost him his life. But Vonnegut is not of course referring to material value. Is war worth the manslaughter? Is it worth the humiliation? Can there be a "Christian reason" to fight and kill and die? Is there anyone at all who benefits from this? Perhaps only spent complacent playboys compensating for their midlife crisis with young women and comfortable research on the backgrounds of war from a comfortable hospital bed like Rumfoord? All this is overlaid by the smell of "mustard gas and roses", the stench of decay.

In Gruppen können die Antworten zu den beiden folgenden Aufgaben formuliert und anschließend vorgetragen werden:

1. What is the most dramatic proof that Vonnegut wants to make us aware that war does not even teach those who suffered in it to learn from it?

   Billy Pilgrim. He seems to have gained no deeper consciousness about war and its atrocities. He neither complains about what he has experienced nor does he despair. He is indifferent, even after so many horrible events and losses (p. 121). The only thing that once enters his mind is that it would be funny or good to be able to rewind occasions like the war and let them run backwards, like that war film he watched the night he was kidnapped by the Tralfamadorians (pp. 74–75).

[1] Die Verbindung mit Hobbes sollte den Schülerinnen und Schüler durch den Religions-, Ethik- oder Geschichtsunterricht möglich sein. Ggf. muss man gezielt darauf hinweisen. Intensiver kann hier wohl kaum auf die Theorie eingegangen werden. Es ist aber interessant, dass Hobbes in seiner Definition von Krieg auch mit dem Begriff der Zeit operiert, die eine andere Eigenschaft erhält („ähnlich dem Wetter") als sie im Frieden hat. (Leviathan, Buch I, ch. XIII)

But the most irritating thing is that he has no scruples in letting his son join the army and enter the Vietnam war. He is even proud to have raised – with some difficulties during early adolescence admittedly – a strong and patriotic Green Beret (p. 20–21). In the novel, we read that that little soldier had already been in his sperm (p. 121). So all the time – no matter how hard, horrible, traumatic, and disgusting the world around him was, how much he suffered, or how ill-treated he was, Billy Pilgrim kept his patriotic conviction. War is still an acceptable human activity for him.
He could, of course, theoretically defend himself against this accusation, claiming that, according to his travels in time, he knows that war cannot be prevented anyway (p. 60). So why then should he stand up at the Lions Club meeting and argue against the positive Vietnam war propaganda (p. 60)?
But we also know that Billy has the mind and soul of a child. He cannot change the present, the past, or the future. So why should he change his attitude, if "everything was fine, and nothing hurt", as Vonnegut would – ironically – adopt the epitaph for himself too (p. 121). Can Billy Pilgrim ever understand? Certainly not, as his name indicates that he is an ever-travelling "pilgrim" not reaching the final destination, the wisdom an ill-treated human being could have gained if he had had the insight.

2. Compare the veterans: Billy Pilgrim and Kurt Vonnegut Jr. What do they have in common and where do they differ?

Both merge into their middle-class life smoothly after their return from war. Billy Pilgrim prospers more than Vonnegut, but the latter is much healthier and does not suffer from having to travel in time.
They are caring family fathers. Both own dogs that are their most valuable friends. They have sons. They differ in how they raise them, however, because Billy Pilgrim is proud of his son becoming a soldier. Vonnegut has warned his sons never ever to engage in war or any other action that might cause massacre or be fatally violent. ("I have told my sons that they are not under any circumstances to take part in massacres … I have also told them not to work for companies which make massacre machinery …" p. 19).
We know that Vonnegut returned to Dresden after the war with his war comrade O'Hare. Billy never mentions if he did or not. His lasting impression of Dresden will be the beetfield on the Elbe outside of Halle (p. 5).
Both can be compared to Don Quixote. Like him, who fights against the windmills, they seem to be fighting a futile battle: Billy Pilgrims tries to bring salvation and consolation to mankind from the Tralfamadorians. No one takes him seriously. He gets treated like a lunatic.
Vonnegut writes a seemingly structurally helter-skelter novel against war, that is like writing an "anti-glacier" novel, as we know from the first chapter. Both Vonnegut and Billy Pilgrim are filled with their message, which is peace like pilgrims in contrast to the martial crusaders. But they both annoy people by the way they are proclaiming it: Billy, by spreading the Tralfamadorian gibberish via the radio, Vonnegut, by using black humour and mocking at holy idols of the Americans at a hyper-sensitive time when the Vietnam war and Cold War against Russia were going on.

Trotz der Anfeindungen und Repressionen hat das Werk einen hohen Stellenwert in der amerikanischen Literatur. Die folgende Information will den Fokus auf das zentrale Anliegen Vonneguts, die Vermeidung weiterer Kriege in der Welt, richten und damit die inhaltliche Besprechung des Werkes beschließen:

Information (Lehrervortrag)

Literary significance of the novel *Slaughterhouse-Five* by Kurt Vonnegut Jr.

In its publication year, *Slaughterhouse-Five* was nominated for a *Nebula* best novel award and for a *Hugo* best novel award, 1970. […] In 1998, the *Modern Library* ranked *Slaughterhouse-Five* **eighteenth** on its list of the 100 best English-language novels of the 20th century. It also appeared in *Time* magazine's list of the 100 best English-language novels written since 1923. The reviews of *Slaughterhouse-Five* have been largely positive since the 31 March 1969 review in *The New York Times* newspaper that glowingly concedes: "you'll either love it, or push it back in the science fiction corner."

Adapted from: http://en.wikipedia.org/wiki/Slaughterhouse-Five, /6.4.13

Would you push it away in the science fiction corner?

Hier können nochmals kurz die Merkmale des Genres, wie sie durchaus vorhanden sind, aber auch die Unterschiede umrissen werden (vgl. Is *Slaughterhouse-Five* – a science fiction novel?, S. 88). Es sollte aber zügig zur Feststellung gekommen werden, dass es eben gerade die brutal realistischen Darstellungen von menschenverachtenden Kriegsereignissen sind, die dem Roman als Zeugnis und Abbild, aber auch als schwarzer Parodie der *conditio humana* Bedeutung verleihen:

1. If it is not a science fiction novel that Vonnegut wanted to give us – what is that "telepathic schizophrenic" conglomeration of a narration then?

   It is a warning for humankind not to make war. The message is only wrapped in that science fiction costume, but the principle is clear and – taught by the Tralfamadorian aliens: the most valuable thing that Billy Pilgrim had learnt from them was "how the inhabitants of a whole planet can live in peace – Earthlings must be the terrors of the Universe" (p. 116–117). Peace is all he wants besides respect for the human being, as he concludes after O'Hare's reading out of the statistics on births and deaths: "I suppose they all want dignity" (p. 212). With an admonishing finger, he points at the human condition and has thus created a reminder of peace that we should take to heart.

2. Let's sum up Vonnegut's intention: do you remember the novel's refrain?

   "So it goes."

3. If you take this refrain as a symbol or code words for Vonnegut's message, what could it stand for ultimately?

so = no it = more goes = war	**Peace!!!**

Die Einheit kann mit einer *zipper activity* abgeschlossen werden.[1] Dazu sollen sich die Schülerinnen und Schüler in zwei Reihen gegenüber aufstellen. Wenn jeder idealerweise einem anderen gegenübersteht, wird das Funktionieren des Reißverschlusses erklärt. Die Reihen werden zunächst A und B genannt. Die Schülerinnen und Schüler erfahren, dass sich auf ein

[1] Zu dieser und weiteren Methoden siehe z. B. Peschel, Alexandra und Schallhorn, Karola, *Method Guide*, Kreative Methoden für den Englischunterricht in der Oberstufe. Schöningh, Paderborn 2004.

Kommando hin die As um ein Gegenüber weiterbewegen sollen. Der „Freigewordene" der B-Reihe reiht sich unten in die As ein usw. Es erfolgt dann jeweils eine Arbeitsanweisung:

> Stand in two lines facing each other. You are Row A – you are Row B. Whenever I clap my hands, Row A moves up one student. The B student left on their own joins the As. This will work like a zipper does. Let's try it.

Das wird zunächst als "Trockenübung" ausprobiert. Wenn es klappt, kommt die Anweisung:

> Remember the little bird chirping its "Poo-tee-weet" at the beginning, in the middle (p. 100), and at the end of the novel? How would you translate its chirp into your own English words now, after knowing the story and its message? Tell your partner what the bird says to Billy Pilgrim!

Die Schülerinnen und Schüler tauschen auf diese Art und Weise viele mögliche Interpretationen aus. Bei jedem Wechselsignal erfahren sie neue Auslegungen. Am Ende des Reißverschlusses, den man je nachdem, wie gut die Aktion von den Schülerinnen und Schüler angenommen und umgesetzt wird, länger oder kürzer laufen lassen kann, werden alle Schülerinnen und Schüler in einen Kreis gebeten.
Die erste Frage sollte eine Metafrage sein, um die Empfindungen der Schülerinnen und Schüler bei dieser Unterrichtsform zu würdigen:

> How did you find the "zipper"? Did you enjoy it? Do you find it meaningful?

Die zweite Frage dient der Auswertung und der Ergebnissicherung:

> Tell me, which interpretation did you like best, of all the ones that you heard?

Nachdem einige Varianten in indirekter Rede mündlich wiedergegeben wurden, dürfen die Schülerinnen und Schüler an ihre Plätze zurückkehren. Sie können den Vogel zeichnen und so viele Ideen, wie ihnen aus dem *zipper* noch in Erinnerung sind, plakativ um das Bild anordnen. Das kann auch an der Tafel geschehen:

"All we are saying is give peace a chance" wäre auch eine mögliche Übersetzung, die sogar den musikalischen Abschluss bilden kann. Der Song hierfür ist „Give peace a chance" vom Peace Choir unter Regie von John Lennon. Im Internet finden sich auch einige Videos zum Titel zur Auswahl.

Component 8

Post-reading activities

Der Film bietet sich zum Vergleich mit der Romanvorlage an. Wie konnte dieses strukturell schwierige Buch in ein umsetzbares Filmdrehbuch umgewandelt werden? Einige der Themen können vertieft werden, besonders wenn ein aktueller Bezug da ist, wie z. B. die Frage, wie Amerika mit seinen Veteranen aus dem Irak- und Afghanistan-Krieg umgeht. Es muss aber nicht nur politisch-ernst bleiben. Das Buch ist ein Produkt der 60er-Jahre in Amerika. Durch den Vietnamkrieg hat sich die legendäre *flower-power*-Hippiekultur ausgebildet. Hier findet sich auch Fröhliches, um ganz in Vonneguts positivem Sinn das Leben optimistisch anzugehen – trotz all der menschengemachten Unbilden. Eine 60er-Jahre-Party kann das Highlight zum Abschluss sein.

Eine allgemeine Evaluation der Lektüre, die den *Reading Companions* beigefügt werden kann, rundet die Romanerarbeitung ab ***(Copy 16 „Likening" the novel, S. 122)***

Einige Vorschläge für *term – papers* oder andere Schülerpräsentationen:

- "Ami go home" – comment on the development of the relationship between Germany and the USA from World War II until today.
- Most people agree that Nazism was truly evil. Was the bombing of Dresden therefore justified?
- As expressed in *Slaughterhouse-Five*, what does Vonnegut see as the possibility for a meaningful life in the modern world?
- From *Slaughterhouse-Five*, would you conclude that Vonnegut is a feminist, or is his admiration for women a form of "male chauvinism"?
- Does Vonnegut's slangy, conversational tone trivialize or strengthen the book's serious points?
- How is authority presented in the novel?
- How does luck figure in Billy Pilgrim's life? Is he a lucky person or an unlucky person? Use examples from the novel to argue your case.
- A flying saucer and little green "Tralfamadorians" – comment on Vonnegut's use of the science fiction elements in the novel against the background of Kennedy's space programme in the 1960s.
- Is *Slaughterhouse-Five* a historical fiction or a science fiction? Write an essay defining each genre and answering this question. Use examples from the text to support your opinion.
- Compare Tralfamadorian views of life and death with different religious philosophies.

Eine Studienfahrt nach Dresden wäre natürlich die optimale Abrundung.

"Likening" the novel

- **Evaluate your reading of the novel. Answer the following questions as preparation for a text to be posted on your internet blog.**

1. State your "liking" on the scale by placing a cross in the appropriate box:

–3	–2	–1	0	1	2	3

Briefly comment your evaluation:

___

___

___

2. Whom did you like best? Why?

___

___

3. Did you dislike anybody? Why?

___

___

4. What do you think about the suspense in the story?

___

___

___

5. What was thrilling?

___

___

6. What was annoying?

___

___

7. Would you recommend the novel to a friend? Why or why not?

___

___

8. If you could ask the author a question or two, what would you want to know?

___

___

Anhang

The USA and the Second World War

A chronology of the historical events relevant in the novel *Slaughterhouse-Five* by Kurt Vonnegut

1937–1940	Japan	Japan invades China. The United States stop the oil and steel trade with Japan. In September 1940, Japan becomes an ally of Nazi Germany and Italy (the Axis alliance). The pact against the USA is drawn up.
1939	Europe	With the German **invasion of Poland** (1 September), the Second World War begins. Two days later, Great Britain and France declare war on Germany. In November, the neutral USA starts exports of arms and munitions to Germany's enemies.
1940	Europe	The **Dunkirk** debacle: a German attack in Belgium takes British and French troops totally by surprise. They flee desperately – it is said, in their underwear ... Belgium, Norway, the Netherlands, France, and Denmark are conquered by the Germans. The Coventry Blitz: the industrial city and its famous cathedral were destroyed in heavy bombings on 14 November. Approximately 568 people lost their lives and almost 900 were badly injured. The Battle of Britain had started in August.
1941	Japan	As a reaction to the trade embargo, Japan occupies southern French Indo-China and blackmails the USA. Negotiations in November fail. On 7 December, Japan attacks the US naval base in Hawaii, **Pearl Harbor**. The Americans were absolutely unprepared, and about 20 ships were sunk or badly damaged. 2343 soldiers and sailors lost their lives. The next day, 8 December, the US declared war on Japan. On 11 December, Germany and Italy, in return, declare war on the US.
1941	Europe	The **Siege of Tobruk** was a confrontation that lasted 241 days between the Axis and Allied forces in North Africa during the Western Desert Campaign of the Second World War. The siege started on 11 April 1941 when Tobruk in Libya was attacked by an Italo–German force under Lieutenant General Erwin Rommel and his *Afrikakorps*. They finally defeated the British army. The Germans invade Russia in June.
1944	Europe	**D-Day**: the invasion of Normandy by the Allied Forces on 6 June to liberate Europe. On 12 September, the signal for the Battle of Germany is given. The **Battle of the Bulge** is a strong counterattack by the Germans. About 77 000 US soldiers are killed in action or imprisoned. The Battle is halted after ten days.
1945	Japan	American and British bombers attack Japan. On 6 August, the US drop the first atomic bomb in history on the city of **Hiroshima**. About 86 000 people, mostly civilians, are killed. The second atomic bomb is released over Nagasaki. This causes the immediate surrender of Japan (10 August–2 September).
1945	Europe	The **Bombing of Dresden** (13–14 February): during the night, about 800 Royal Air Force bombers drop tons of high explosives and 650 000 incendiaries on the old city. The bombing continues the next day while firestorms rage. US and Russian troops meet at Torgau on the Elbe on 24 April. **V-Day**: 8 May is the date of the official end of the war in Europe. Germany has surrendered the day before.

1954	Vietnam	**Division of Vietnam**: the north gets support from the USSR in order to strengthen the Communist system. The south receives support from the USA to preserve an anti-Communist regime in Asia.
1956	Vietnam	Civil war. The US send troops on a mission to defend Vietnam's "freedom".
1962	Vietnam	President **J F Kennedy** officially orders military participation by US forces.
1965	Vietnam	The US troops fight against two fronts in Vietnam: they are not only fighting against the Communist north but also against a group of South Vietnamese Communist rebels, the Viet Cong, attacking them within the country they want to protect. When the Vietcong kills eight American soldiers in February1965, President Lyndon Johnson starts Operation Rolling Thunder and orders the direct bombing of selected targets in North Vietnam. The number of troops sent to Vietnam has increased to 184 000 by the end of the year. The first anti-war protests take place in the USA.
1967	USA	In June 1967, six Vietnam war veterans found the **Vietnam Veterans Against the War Organization**, which today still campaigns for peace, justice, and the rights of all United States military veterans.
1967	Vietnam	Peace talks fail. The bombing escalates.
1968	Vietnam	The **Tet Offensive**: massive attacks by the North Vietnamese make the USA realize its enemy is tougher than estimated. 515 000 US soldiers are fighting in Vietnam now. In the **My Lai Massacre**, US troops kill about 500 South Vietnamese civilians. About 145 000 US soldiers are killed in action.
1968	USA	By now, the majority of the American **public opposes the war**. The war costs nearly $30 000 million a year. Johnson is under pressure especially by the American liberals and restricts the bombing. He declares that he will not run for elections again. 4 April 1968: **Dr. Martin Luther King** is assassinated.
1969	Cambodia	Peace negotiations fail again. Communist strongholds in Cambodia are bombed.
1970	USA	**Protests in America** are brutally beaten down with four students killed in Ohio and two more in Mississippi. Despite the increasing number of protestors, even among members of Congress, President Richard Nixon defends his strategy, which is to gradually hand control of the war over to the South Vietnamese and continue to bomb Cambodia.
1973	Vietnam	A **peace treaty** is signed by North Vietnam, South Vietnam, and the Provisional Revolutionary Government (the Viet Cong).
1975	Vietnam	**Saigon**: the North Vietnamese seize Saigon as US helicopters rescue about 1 100 Americans and 5 500 South Vietnamese.

CD contents and book references[1]

CD	Title	Length	Book (chapter/page)
1/1	Harper Audio Presents Slaughterhouse-Five	12:21	Front page, Dedication, Poem, etc. I / 0 – 8
1/2	While I was studying to be an anthropologist …	11:31	I / 8 – 14
1/3	O'Hare and I gave up on remembering …	11:44	I / 15 – 22
1/4	Listen …	11:35	II / 23 – 30
1/5	And so on …	11:21	II / 30 – 37
1/6	Now, lying in the ditch …	14:58	II / 37 – 45
2/1	Billy blinked in 1965 …	10:56	II / 45 -51
2/2	The Germans and the dog …	14:54	III / 52 – 61
2/3	Billy owned a lovely …	09:43	III / 61 – 67
2/4	Billy Pilgrim was packed …	05:42	III / 67 -71
2/5	Billy Pilgrim could not sleep …	12:49	IV / 72 – 80
2/6	Listen – on the tenth night …	10:41	IV / 80 – 86
2/7	Billy Pilgrim says that …	07:00	V / 87 – 91
3/1	As the Americans were waiting …	09:07	V / 91 – 96
3/2	Billy Pilgrim was on fire …	13:20	V / 96 – 105
3/3	Now the head Englishman …	09:50	V / 105 – 111
3/4	And Billy travelled in time …	12:47	V / 111 – 119
3/5	The honeymoon was taking place …	12:27	V / 119 – 128
3/6	While the British colonel …	11:00	V / 128 – 135
4/1	Listen: Billy Pilgrim says …	12:48	VI / 136 – 143
4/2	Billy and Lazzaro and poor old Edgar Derby …	06:14	VI / 143 – 147
4/3	The temperature climbed startlingly …	10:29	VI / 147 – 153
4/4	Billy Pilgrim got onto a chartered plane …	11:28	VII / 154 – 161
4/5	The Americans in the slaughterhouse …	09:07	VIII / 162 – 167
4/6	Billy Pilgrim parked his Cadillac …	10:32	VIII / 167 – 173
4/7	People drifted away now …	08:50	VIII / 173– 178
5/1	"Tell me a story", Montana Wildhack said …	05:43	VIII / 178 – 181
5/2	Here's how Billy Pilgrim lost his wife …	08:28	IX / 182 – 186
5/3	One of the books Lily had brought	08:26	IX / 186 – 191
5/4	"Americans have finally heard about Dresden …"	09:43	IX / 191 – 197

[1] CD*: Kurt Vonnegut, Slaughterhouse-Five or the Children's Crusade: A Duty Dance With Death.* Performed by Ethan Hawk, unabridged, includes an interview with the author and an archival author recording set to music, 6 hours , 5 CDs, 2003, Harper/Collins Publishers, Caedmon, USA; Book edition: Kurt Vonnegut*: Slaughterhouse-Five*, Dell Publishing, New York, [1]1969; 2007

CD	Title	Length	Book (chapter/page)
5/5	Later on, as a middle-aged optometrist ...	19:22	IX /197 -209
5/6	Robert Kennedy, whose summer home ...	09:52	X / 210 -215
5/7	Kurt Vonnegut interview	10:20	[Audio-transcript see *Appendix*]
5/8	Tick Tock	07:26	[The coming of the saucer – text excerpt set with music]

Weiterführende Literatur und Medien

- Fleischmann, Alice, *„So it goes"?:* Trauma und *false memory* in Kurt Vonneguts „Slaughterhouse-Five", München: Grin-Verlag, Dez. 2011
- Freese, Peter [Hrsg.]: *Der Roman im Englischunterricht der Sekundarstufe II*: Theorie und Praxis / Peter Freese ; Liesel Hermes (Hrsg.). – Paderborn : Schöningh, 1977
- Freese, Peter: *The Clown of Armageddon*: the novels of Kurt Vonnegut / Peter Freese. – Heidelberg: Winter, 2009
- Kuppels, Dominik: *Krieg und „schwarzer Humor". Postmoderne Erzählverfahren bei Joseph Heller (Catch-22), Kurt Vonnegut (Slaughterhouse-five) und Thomas Pynchon (Gravity's rainbow).* Tectum, Marburg 1997 (= Edition Wissenschaft; Reihe Anglistik 16)
- Merrill Robert and Peter A. Scholl, *Vonnegut's Slaughterhouse-Five*: The Requirements of Chaos, in *Studies in American Fiction,* Vol. 6, No. 1, Spring, 1978
- Möller, Olaf, *Schlachthof 5*, Booklet, DVD, Koch Media 2008
- Peschel, Alexandra und Schallhorn, Karola: *Method Guide*, Kreative Methoden für den Englischunterricht in der Oberstufe, Paderborn: Schöningh 2004
- Pinternagel, Stefan T.: *Kurt Vonnegut jr. und die Science Fiction – Kilgore Trout, Tralfamadore und Bokononismus.* Berlin: Shayol 2005
- Regler, Marc, *Constructing "Slaughterhouse-Five"*: The Interplay between Fiction, Reality, Structure and Time, München: Grin-Verlag, Juli 2007
- Schatt, Stanley: "Kurt Vonnegut, Jr., *Chapter 4: Vonnegut's Dresden Novel: Slaughterhouse-Five.*", In *Twayne's United States Authors Series Online*. New York: G. K. Hall & Co., 1999. Previously published in print in 1976 by Twayne Publishers
- Smith, Dennis Stanton: *Slaughterhouse-Five,* Wiley Publishing Inc., 1997
- Wagenseil, Kurt [Übers.]: *Schlachthof 5*, Kurt Vonnegut, Jr., Rowohlt, Reinbek bei Hamburg, 1972

Internet

- http://www.vonnegutlibrary.org/; The Guardian, Friday 13 April 2007/17.10.12
- http://www.guardian.co.uk/books/2011/dec/03/kurt-vonnegut-biography?INTCMP=ILCNETTXT3487/ (17.10.2012)
- http://www.nndb.com/people/928/000022862/12.2.2013 [Kurt Vonnegut]
- www.britannica.org
- Sturm, Daniel: „Local vet recalls his POW days with the late Kurt Vonnegut 2007–05–03" by Daniel Sturm Athens NEWS Contributor *auf* „Indiana Military Organization" http://www.indianamilitary.org/ – German POW Camps – Slaughterhouse-Five- Vonnegut, Karl [sic!] (25.5.2013)
- Teaching the Vietnam War. (The Vietnam Conflict) Part 1. Some suggested lesson plans and approaches By John J. Fitzgerald fitzgera@comcast.net (22.4.2013)

- http://en.wikipedia.org/wiki/Slaughterhouse-Five (6.4.2013)
- http://en.wikipedia.org/wiki/Slaughterhouse-Five (6.4.2013)
- www.einestages.spiegel.de (6.4.2013)
- http://www.history.com/topics/battle-of-the-bulge (22.4.2013)
- http://www.gensuikin.org/english/photo.html (22.4.2013)
- http://www.indianamilitary.org/ – German POW Camps – Slaughterhouse-Five- Vonnegut, Karl [sic!] (25.5.2013) Viele Kameraden von Vonnegut, die mit ihm im Schlachthof in Dresden gefangen waren, haben hier ausführliche Veteranen-Berichte eingestellt.
- http://www.schuleplus.de/Englisch/films/filmanalysis-language.htm (16.4.2013)
- www.songtexte.com (22.4.2013)
- http://www.vanishedamericana.com/old-time-fun/yon-yonson-1899–stage-play-poster/ (4.2.2013)
- http://yeli.us/Flash/Fire.html (Billy Joel song: We didn't start the fire/22.4.2013)

CD

- Kurt Vonnegut, *Slaughterhouse-Five or the Children's Crusade*: A Duty Dance with Death, performed by Ethan Hawke, unabridged, includes an interview with the author and an archival author recording set to music. Caedmon, Harper AudioStudios, 2003

Filme

- Schlachthof 5 – (Slaughterhouse-Five), Koch Media 2008 (Regie: George Roy Hill; original music Glenn Gould; Universal Studios, 1972)

Weitere Filmvorschläge

- Terra X Vol.10, *Der Kreuzzug der Kinder* u. a., Universum GmbH, frei ab 12, 2009
- *Hair*, frei ab 6, Regie: Milos Forman, 2001
- *Die letzte Schlacht, Battle of the Bulge.* (Achtung: nicht verwechseln mit anderen Filmen, die auch „Die letzte Schlacht" heißen!) Regie Ken Annakin, 1965
- *Amerikas Kriege,* Spiegel TV (Nr. 22), 2010
- *Als der Krieg nach Deutschland kam.* Spiegel TV (Nr. 23), 2005
- *Apocalypse Now,* frei ab 16, Regie: Francis Ford Coppola, 2000
- *Born on the Fourth of July.* 2 Oscars, Regie: Oliver Stone, 2003
- *The Deer Hunter* (dt. „Die durch die Hölle gehen"). Regie: Michael Cimino, 1978
- *Full Metal Jacket,* frei ab 16, Regie: Stanley Kubrick, 2001
- *Platoon,* frei ab 16, Regie: Oliver Stone, 2005
- *Soldier James Ryan,* frei ab 16, Regie: Steven Spielberg, 2002
- *The Life of Brian*, Monty Python, frei ab 12, Regie: Terry Jones, 1979

Songs and their topical relevance

- The Cars: *Let the good times roll (*Tralfamadorian philosophy, author's message)
- Dire Straits: *Brothers in arms* (anti-war)
- Hardcastle, Paul: *19* (children as soldiers, Vietnam war, anti-war)
- Joel, Billy: *We didn't start the fire* (social criticism, America's global rule, massacre, war)
- OMD [Orchestral Manoeuvres in the Dark]: *Dresden*
- Peace Choir: *Give peace a chance* (Tralfamadorian philosophy, author's message)
- Rogers, Kenny: *Ruby, don't take your love to town* (war injured veteran's fate)
- Scorpions: *Still loving you* (time)
- Status Quo: *You're in the army now* (anti-war, naïve idea about a soldier's life)
- Wishful Thinking: *Hiroshima*

Bildnachweis

S. 3, 23, 45: Verlagsarchiv Schöningh/Igeldesign – S. 6, 52: © picture-alliance/dpa – S. 41: © 1985 CHRYSALIS RECORDS LTD., Oval Music – S. 44: © privat – S. 45: © Verlagsarchiv Schöningh/Domke – S. 62: Verlagsarchiv Schöningh/Kassing